IS-BEING

The Spiritual Evolution

Mel Cross

Love and blessings,

Mel

x

Cover designed by Mel Cross

Mel Cross
Visit my website at
www.mel-cross.co.uk
www.is-being.com

Printed in the United States of America

First Printing: October 2019
Amazon

ISBN- 9781697582178

*To the brightest and most beautifully perfect light I
found deep within the darkness...
With your hand in mine I found my soul.
Through tears, fears, separation, love and laughter,
and even in the bleakest and blackest of times,
we never let go.*

*You showed me love.
You showed me faith.
You showed me trust.
You showed me truth.
You showed me surrender.
You showed me stillness.
You showed me humility.*

*Your light is within me and mine within you.
Thank you for holding my hand and walking with me,
and in me.
One light...
Two hearts...
As it always has been, as it is, and how it always will be.
From the beginning, until the end.
I love you*

For that which 'Is'.
For spirit.
For the human angels who have walked with me, held my hand, questioned me, made me laugh, made me cry, brought wisdom, illumination, and experiences both positive and negative. For those who brought friendship, hugs and love. For those who picked me up when I fell, for those who listened, and for those who challenged me and helped me grow. And, for the angels who have stood by my side, no matter what.
For those who brought their own experiences and knowledge to the table and have worked hard to apply the understanding within this book to their own lives, so that they too may shine and be an example to us all.
For those who have helped me in bringing this work together, supporting me and advising me from their own areas of expertise.
For the angels with the dirtiest wings who work in the darkest and most unimaginable of places, who take their light, like stars, to those in need of guidance, vision and protection.
For the angels who work in the light, shining like the sun, illuminating and guiding each and every one of us.
And for the wisest, kindest, funniest, most loving and greatest of teachers, the angels I am blessed to call my children.

TESTIMONIALS

Our spiritual life is a unique journey to the infinite. It is like climbing to the top of the hill where we discover our with the infinite, and with all. But our starting points at the bottom of the hill are different and unique. The way we experience the infinite, which Mel calls IS-BEING, is unique. In this book Mel describes her own unique journey and her own unique experience and thus invites everyone to make his or her own unique journey and unique experience of IS-BEING. It is a very original, creative and inspiring journey and discovery, described with almost humility and love. I wish and hope that everyone who reads this book may be inspired to take his or her spiritual journey and discover the infinite in a unique way.

Br. John Martin Sahajananda
Author of 'You are the Light' (2003), 'What is truth' (2013), 'Fully Human – Fully Divine' (2014) and more

A masterful and prophetic revelation of a new spiritual epoch. Whilst religion can provide us with a traditional framework for the spiritual journey, *Is-Being* takes us beyond the limits of the human mind into an entirely different operating system. This paradigm shift in human consciousness and evolution reveals how the energetic and vibratory resonance of the heart is the doorway into an enlightened presence rooted in pure reality!

Richard Wiltshire
Salvos Chaplain

This is a labour of love - literally. Mel Cross writes with clarity, compassion and refreshing self-honesty, in a structured down-to-earth way ...speaking quietly with those now beginning to wake, and with those already living in healingful ways with heart-centred consciousness of 'that which Is'. Mel introduces the loving essence and transformative power of *true* spirituality... with illuminating words seemingly designed to dissolve the endemic egoic fearfulness that causes so much disconnection, division and distortion in our world, and all kinds of self-confining fog. This powerfully gentle stirring piece of writing calls to us to come together as *One* ...in our own quiet ways, you and I.

Jaimie Cahlil
Transpersonal psychotherapist & artist

'Is-Being' is a refreshing take on the 'spiritual' understanding of life which tries to avoid the pitfalls of traditional language and the misunderstandings, conflicts, and problems that different interpretations of meaning can lead us into. This is a book for anyone who wants to go beyond doctrine and theology into a real human understanding of 'what is.' It draws on various aspects of energetic healing and psychology and also the universal perennial wisdom stream that underlies all good spiritual teaching, but defines mostly its own terms rather than using established ones, which gives it a fresh feel.

Revd Don MacGregor
Author of 'Blue Sky God: The Evolution of Science and Spirituality.'

Defining a new Heart-Centred spiritual language for an awakened collective, with imperative insights into soul, spirit and guides, the clarity and conviction with which Cross delivers this essential information is a triumph.

The illumination into unshakable Faith and Trust which Cross invites us is truly empowering; for beginners and even the most experienced spiritual pioneers.

Cross enables us to feel a deeper sense of humility inspiring us to help others within this incredible and infinitely beautiful connected vastness of that which 'Is'.

Will Reardon
Multidimensional Artist and Angelic Reiki Master Teacher

Mel Cross writes with conviction, passion and clarity of message, but there is no ritual here, no dogma, there isn't even a god if you don't want to bring one with you. What you'll find is an intensely personal spirituality that encourages us to shed the unnecessary and harmful clutter from our individual lives, so we might reconnect with what is most important for us and for the world.

Mark Youd
Artist

Is-being is a truly thoughtful, special book. The words have been carefully considered and have such depth and compassion behind them. The artwork and poetry throughout the book help to deepen the sense of personal development. It has been wonderful to read and connect to the heart and to inclusivity - what I love the most is it feels very accessible no matter what religion or faith one may have!

Robin Watkins-Davis
Founder of Bliss by Robin and Bliss.Ed – Sharing yoga and empowering young people to improve mental health
Artist – Producer of SHIFT

I feel there is a huge challenge to our contemporary world to find a language which opens the spiritual depths of experience and meaning to those who are seeking such insight. This book does just that, in that the author carefully explores the malaise of meaninglessness and lasting connection using language that remains open and inviting, across culture/religion/age/and experience. It will nourish and encourage the reader into spaces with themselves where the sense of connectedness to all created matter, and indeed to the great ONENESS beyond can be realised. The reader is supported in this inner journey by illustrations which can hold moments of reflection as the experience during reading unfolds. It is a huge canvas, but its insights are incremental and presented to the reader as reminders of the destination to which they are moving.

Monica Butler R.S.M.
Religious Sisters of Mercy

There are few words that have been more talked about than "Soul" and "Spirit", yet so little understood. Drawing on her own personal experience, Mel Cross lifts here the veil of confusion to reveal a vivid depiction of our spiritual journey. The clarity of her understanding offers the reader deep insights into the working of the soul. This book represents a most unique guide for any of us to venture further and with renewed confidence onto our path.

Dr Gerald Deshais
Director, The Cotswolds Juice Retreat

Mel's book is a sparkling true light of how we can all be our true selves and share in each other that which has been in all of us since the beginning of time. To love and be loved. To just be. I couldn't put the book down and read it cover to cover and reread parts again. I'm very proud and honoured to call Mel my friend - through this book Mel will become your friend too. Through all of us just being - we can achieve anything and everything. Just follow your heart.

John Clifford

IS-BEING – is a book that has changed my life by giving me clarification, confirmation, understanding and the tools to help me on my own path of BEING. This book is beautifully written, and you can feel the honesty, truthfulness and most of all LOVE from the Author. This book is for everyone no matter what belief system you may have, I thoroughly recommend.

Stephen Wiles
Autism Specialist & Spiritual Guide

Wow, when reading this book, it felt like validation. I felt such a connection, as each time I put the book down and picked it back up, it would validate what I felt was true or what I had just been through.
The book is written for all, as we are all the same yet different.
Our journey is unique, yet the same. Love and light 'Is' the answer.
This has been, and is, what I have always felt.

Charly Holly Jade Tillson
Assistant Team Manager
Learning Disabilities

IMAGES

The images within this book can be pondered upon, meditated with, or used as tools for reflection and contemplation should you choose to stop with them for a while. It may help in absorbing and integrating that which you read, by letting it flow slowly into understanding, through time spent in stillness.

They are from works created as part of my 'Creativity, Spirituality and Surrender' series of paintings and are pure expressions of the dynamic, creative that which 'Is'.

The text below is the extract from this exhibition which took place years before the writing of this book. It was the outcome in a visual form of the exploration of creation and spirituality at a personal level. This strand of questioning, when pulled through further, became part of the catalyst for the process written about in this book.

'The perfect moment of creation is the moment of silent perfection which is just before the illumination of a thought; an idea; a revelation. The silence before the first note, the motionless moment before the pencil scribes paper and paintbrush slides deliciously into paint.

That is the perfection and true magic of creation. It is the 'no-thingness', the infinite void of potential from where all things come. That is the divinity of creation – the moment 'before'...

Once the first note is played, the first line drawn, the first brush stroke swept, the moment is gone.

When the creative moment is transferred into the physical the beauty of perfection diminishes... So how do we capture true intangible creative potential in the physical world? An honest expression of true creative potential would be to just sit, in silence, in 'no thought'. A conduit for the creative spark to feed in to, and through, and into form... A pipe...

To try to control, direct or influence the process muddies the crystal-clear flow. To direct with intent and 'mind' causes the output to be contrived and inauthentic. So, allowing the process to flow and bring 'no-thing' naturally into form, is to be truly creative. It is to surrender to the process. It is to sacrifice one's own desires and thoughts and allow uninfluenced creation to pour forth.

How long can that moment be held? How long can one facilitate the manifestation into the physical without influencing it? Is it seconds, or can it be maintained for longer? Is it sustained by one's ability to surrender, to 'be', and to exist for as long as possible in the 'zone'?

The act of surrender, I believe, is similar to the act of surrender one needs to connect to one's spiritual nature. To surrender, to trust and to allow the process to bring a connection to the divine. Forcing this process pushes the desired illumination of one's spiritual nature further away. To force spiritual or creative connection pushes it away. Allowing, surrendering, trusting and sacrificing one's own thoughts and desires gives space and allowance of flow into the conscious mind... But physically capturing, translating and expressing true creativity and true spirituality is tricky.

The perfection is the connection...

The creation of form from that connection is so clumsy, so inadequate, so primitive and so utterly futile it seems pointless. But still we creatives quest to express. Whether it is in images, music or words, we are compelled to continue.

We need to express this beautiful space from which all things emerge...'

CONTENTS

TO BEGIN

An introduction

We believe we live in a world full of despair and destruction, of pain, corruption and greed. A world where the hungry go unfed, the vulnerable go unheard, and the conflict between peoples at all levels of existence, and in all places, rumble on like blackest thunder. A world where the air, water and earth of the planet are polluted and ravaged, the trees slashed down, and the animals crushed. A world of pain, a world of disharmony, a world of hate. A world where corruption and poison have spread and seeped into every area of life, everywhere that we look, spreading silent and unseen. A world, some say, which cannot be helped, cannot be saved and cannot be put right.

People do not know how to help, do not know how to change, do not know how to bring the light back in to all things. They hide within their lives, and their created worlds, and do not wish to see the truth of that which threatens us all. We have been blinded to our ability to make a difference, to see a different way, to be the difference. We have lost our ability to connect to our truth, the world's truth, the truth of that which 'Is'. We have lost sight, lost direction and worst of all lost hope. The hope that things can change. The hope that the sun, one day, will shine again.

But there is hope. There always has been. There always will be.

It is the glimmering wisp of light in the blackest of places. It is contained within the beat of our heart and each breath that we take. It is the movement of love within all things, between all things, and through all things. It has always been there. It will always be there. Because it 'Is'.

This work is the story of how we can illuminate the light of hope, through the flame of love, and all play our part in the change and evolution people, and the world, so desperately needs.

◆ ◆ ◆

When we are conceived we are a light, pure, and full of potential. We are the gift of life from the eternal sea of potential. The sea from which all things come, and to which all things will return. The sea of infinite possibility. This sea of infinite possibility and infinite potential is where that which 'Is' resides.

Where there is no-thing there is everything.

We come from the no-thing, and we have the potential for the everything. The unique spark of life which we are, the unique facet, the individual aspect of the multifaceted diamond of that which 'Is', shines brightly in that moment of creation.

We are pure energy, pure potential, pure light, pure love.

From that moment on the light that we are begins to become cloaked, covered, solidified and stagnant. Every thought, every experience, everything we think, and everything we do, begins to solidify an identity which we believe to be us around the unique divine light that we are. The pure vibration of divine light begins to be shrouded, and its vibration lowered, to fit in with the illusion created by our environment, our upbringing, society, culture, and us. We are moulded into acceptability and sameness. Our unique light is dulled, coated, and eventually built around, so that we hardly sense it there at all. We have been made blind to that which we truly are, and we can only identify with the outer carapace of the physical, emotional and mental aspects of humanness. We believe that that which we see in the mirror, and the mind-chatter we hear inside our head, are who we truly are.

And this is so very far from the truth.

We then begin to walk through life, searching, looking for answers. We feel the dull ache within our heart, and sense something crucial is missing. We try to fill this perceived void with false identity, status, belongings, relationships and money. We try to bind it with the plasters of religion or belief systems. Our religion and beliefs can help us greatly, as they bring us guidance, support, love and connection. But sometimes they do not uncover the cause of the problem, and do not always wholly help us to deal with it.

We believe the ache to be a 'lack' of something; we feel something is missing in us, or in our lives. But the ache we feel is not lack, it is the ache of what is already there, deep inside us, waiting to be heard. There, waiting to be recognised as the true essence of us is our truth, our soul, and within this our unique light, our connection to that which 'Is'.

We search, and search, and search. We look 'out there' or 'above' us for the answers. We go to gurus and sacred places, we travel, we read, we ask that which 'Is' to give us answers.

But we do not listen.

What we do not realise is that we have all the answers, we are all the answers, we connect to all the answers, and that our connection to that which 'Is' lies deep within our own hearts.

That which 'Is' is inside you – and you are part of that which 'Is'.

This divine truth has been with us always. We have just become unable to see, sense and feel this. We have become unable to connect to our own essential nature, our own truth, our own light. The ache that we feel is not lack, it is us, knocking at our own door to understanding and connection. It is us, trying to be heard.

Therefore, when we consciously connect to, and integrate, our true essential nature and light, we connect to that which 'Is' inside us. We

3

become aware that we are connected to and are part of that which 'Is' above, and we sense peace, light and love within this. We also sense that we flow with the dynamic, creative, no-thing 'Is', which is within, through and around, all things. It is here we connect to all that is, all that was, and all that will be.

> We are not separate, we are not below, we are part of.
> There is no hierarchy to climb to reach that which 'Is', there are no rules, there are no exclusions.
> We are all part of the Whole; each and every one of us.

We do not need answers, we already have everything we need. We just need questions; many, many questions; so that we can be guided on the path to the *Truth* of us. We need to remove the barriers, coatings, imprints, conditioning, and manipulation, which has solidified to become false us. We need to strip ourselves back in every way, until our true light shines and our true connection to that which 'Is' is revealed.

This truth and understanding of the divine connection within is nothing new, as it has been understood and worked towards in many faiths, beliefs and traditions. It has been felt in many ways, at many times, and by many peoples. It has been glimpsed by some, achieved by few, and spoken about by many. But something seems to be happening at this present time. A new way, a new understanding, a new paradigm. The old ways and methods of trying to connect can still be worked with, but the time has come for a new understanding and purity of connection.

The vibration of the planet is raising into love. As a part of this, the call to connect to that which 'Is', and one's own divine essence, is being heard loudly by many who have previously had no interest in religion, or their own spiritual nature. It is as if they have woken up, their blinkers removed, now feeling a strong and relentless urge to sit within their own light and feeling the need to help others to connect to, and sense, their own lights too.

This way of being is exciting, ecstatic, liberating and love-filled, but it does have its downfalls. It can sometimes come with a feeling of isolation, as often individuals are unable to find others who are like them. Sometimes there is fear as the changes, sensations, and understanding, which they now find themselves with, leaves them feeling they are going insane. They become extremely tired for no reason, have vivid dreams, unusual physical sensations and hear and see things differently to how they did before.

These individuals are suddenly finding themselves 'awake', being able to heal, to sense, and to understand their spiritual natures in very profound and intense ways. They are changing their lives, and leaving jobs, relationships, and material belongings. They are changing their diets, stopping smoking or taking drugs, and spontaneously giving up alcohol. They are trying to cleanse themselves, and their lives, to give space to, and accommodate, this new understanding, this new light. They are quite literally becoming their own temples of light. But temples with wide-open doors, allowing the light to flow through them, and out into the world.

The uplifting into love, or raising of vibration, within these individuals, is taking place as a catalyst for recognising the desperate need for change and understanding, at every level of existence.

The world, and everyone in it, need to make changes to themselves, and as a result this will positively affect every other living being, creature, flora, fauna, mineral and non-living thing.

This raising of vibration brings the illumination of the interconnectedness of all things, the Oneness of all things, and the Truth, which is that that which 'Is', is within each and every one of us.

That which 'Is' is in all things, through all things, around all things, and IS all things.

That which 'Is' is in the space between, within the no-thing.
Where there is no-thing, there is everything.
Infinite potential.

That which 'Is' is within us.

It is the duty of those who are aware of what is happening, to help those who are awakening, by supporting, nurturing, guiding and protecting them as they move further and further along their paths. There needs to be somewhere for them to share information, somewhere for them to receive and give love, and somewhere to feel a sense of belonging. A community; a gathering together of people, from all faiths and no faiths.

Everyone welcome. All colours, all ages, all sexualities, all peoples...

Yes, all of us, the beautiful, unique, individuals.
Yes us, the magnificently perfectly-imperfect humans.
Yes us, the physically incarnate soul-lights.
Yes us, the Is-beings living the human being experience.

From this community, the love, light and understanding will be shared. From this community the love, light and understanding will spread further and further, touching more and more people. This in turn will raise the vibration of these new individuals into love, and this will affect everything around each of these individuals. And on, and on it goes, until the new way reaches everyone and everything, and we understand that we are all One.

What the one does, affects the whole.

And we will see how each of us can make a difference, if we truly find our light within,

and truly connect with that which 'Is'.

This new understanding and new way do not negate any faith or belief system, because it is part of them. It is taking place in all faiths and within all beliefs, as well as in places of no faith and no beliefs.

It is an understanding and wisdom which permeates all things, and is a fundamental divine Truth.

God 'Is'.
I 'Am'.

You may wonder how I know this and how I can speak with any wisdom about the above understanding. Is it regurgitated books, belief systems, information passed to me by gurus, or read upon the internet? No.

Everything you find within this book comes via my connection with the dynamic flow of that which 'Is', with the love from that which 'Is', and due to the integration of my soul, and the light of that which 'Is' within this.

Of course, I have explored life, have read, and have learned. Of course, the whole world has permeated my knowledge and understanding as I have travelled my path through life. But my true understanding of the essential nature of all that 'Is', has come about through the removal of blocks, veils and misperception. It has come about through wiping away all that I knew, and all that I was, and starting afresh and in purity; the purity of divine communion.

Through love, faith, trust, truth, surrender, stillness, humility, gratitude, listening, humour, and unwavering determination not to lose focus, no matter how horrendous things became, I walked the path; and these were the only tools I carried with me.

They are the only tools you need.

By *being*, and *listening*, I put total faith in what I was shown, and the way was rolled out, step by step, in-front of me. I was given instruction and I was guided in my understanding. My knowledge of energy work grew as I was given experiences, trials and tests. In faith, love and humility I continued.

This instruction led me through the process of heart-space connection, to energetically dissolve my created-self, to consciously connect my incarnate spirit-self to my soul, to reintegrating my spirit-self into my soul, and to become a pure vessel in which soul could fully incarnate.

Throughout this process, through love and faith, a stronger and stronger connection to that which 'Is' grew. My journey has now continued beyond this process for me to be able to share it with you.

This process and understanding were given to me to share with all of you, with purest love, in purest light, from that which 'Is'.

There are echoes and reflections of the things that I say in all cultures and beliefs, and in both current and past thinking; and, of course, there would be. These things have all been said before, in many ways, and many, many times. But the purity of what has been said has been taken, owned, compartmentalised and solidified into a stagnant and non-fluid way of being. The capturing of the very essence of the teachings, and creating rules and ownership, has alienated the truth from many individuals in the world. We have been told there are rules which must be obeyed, exemptions from who can participate in connecting to that which 'Is', and hierarchy. We have been told we must adhere to the rules and rigidity of that which is presented before us. But this is all an illusion by those who rule, to keep those who don't, disconnected from their true divine nature. It keeps us striving for a perceived, unobtainable goal. We strive to reach towards and hold the hand of that which 'Is', but we have been kept from it. This has created anger, separation and disillusion. Many have turned their back on 'God' and tried to satiate their longing in false and unfulfilling ways. But the time has come, and the longing for change and connection is now felt so deeply, by so many, that things must change. We need to help those who are ready, to strip away everything, and reveal their light within. Then they can shine and light the way for others, so they too can find their way out of the darkness.

With my understanding of the process, and by being within the flowing information of that which 'Is', I will do my best to help guide, support and illuminate those who feel the call.

But the work will be done by you, for you to facilitate the change humanity and the world so desperately needs.

We are One, and together we can do this.

Mel Cross

'IS', 'AM' AND 'ME'

An explanation of words

For our minds to be able to grasp that which our heart already understands, and *knows* at the deepest level, we must use words. And words are the calcification of that which is behind, and beyond, words and description. This bringing into form through the making of a sound (a word), to describe that which is indescribable, is the first cause of inadequate communication. There are no words to describe what is behind them, therefore, to try to explain that which 'Is', through a series of random man-made sounds, we find we have already stumbled.

That which 'Is' can only be experienced, not explained.

The second problem with words is that they are open to misinterpretation, and they can be misconstrued. Words are only processed by the mind, using that which has given meaning to the word, i.e. circumstance, conditioning, experience and teaching. The word can only then be interpreted in context, by the 'rules' and understanding the mind has placed upon the word.

One word can vary in its meaning, understanding, and emotional force, according to an individual's upbringing, culture, teachings, experiences, societal circumstance and media manipulation. A single word can be interpreted in a huge variety of ways and can create a multitude of emotional reactions; both positive and negative.

So now we have a word which is insufficient to describe the indescribable, and infinitely misinterpreted by those who use it, because of the individual's understanding of the word, due to the variables around which the word was internalised.

An individual using the word believes his interpretation and understanding of the word to be 'correct', and because we work from the 'Me', rather than from our 'Am', we work with our 'Created-self'. Our created-self always likes to be right and superior, including the usage of a single word. Therefore, we will fight with those whose understanding of a word varies from our own interpretation and understanding of that word. This causes rifts between individuals, groups and indeed countries and belief systems.

So now we have a word which is describing the indescribable, interpreted in different ways, and fought about because we work from mind-space rather than heart-space.

The fourth issue with the word is that when that which seeks to be expressed is calcified into it, the word has already lost its meaning and its life. It becomes solid, ownable, interpretable by human *mind*, and begins to decompose. The energy which brought it into being has moved into form, and this solidification loses its sparkle and life.

Without words and definition things are fluid, constantly forming and re-forming, fresh, light-filled and alive. When things are not defined, they can be infinitely expressed and individually felt, rather than thought. It is only our minds which need definition – our heart-space lives fully in the infinite beauty of flow.

Our minds need to define, our hearts sense and feel. Meaning is felt rather than thought.

When we remove the words, we are left with the Truth of things.
The Truth of things is where we need to be.

Human beings have defined and redefined things. They have interpreted and misinterpreted. They have owned things by definition. They have used words and their interpretation, to supress, to create hierarchy, to create structure, society and religion. All using words. Words which cannot accurately describe the indescribable, which are misinterpreted and interpreted according to manipulated context. Whose meanings are fought about due to working from the mind (Me), rather than the heart-space (Am), and are in a constant state of entropy due to the calcifying nature of capturing the uncapturable into form. So, we are already in confusion about how to express that which needs to be expressed but cannot be defined; and that which needs to be interpreted, when things are ultimately misinterpreted.

Writing this book is indeed counterproductive to that which wishes to be understood, but, as we are at the starting point of true understanding, we need to give some form of knowledge to the mind. By doing this we can then move away from the mind, and begin to work with the Truth, which is contained within the heart-space.

So, in a manner of speaking, we need to read this book, then put it on the library shelf within the mind. It is to be dipped into and lived, rather than memorised and thought.

It is to be known, then unknown.

Held, and then let go of.

The information is never to be *owned*, and not to be definitive.

This book, when written at another time and in another place, would perhaps be totally different; this is the beauty of seeking to express the ultimately indefinable, from the place of infinite possibility. And that is how it should be.

These words are the futile scribing of one human's interpretation of the indefinable, as it was presented into my conscious awareness. Perhaps the next book will be totally different. And this is the joy of working with the *flow* rather than the *fact*.

I go a long way to discuss words, but there is a reason for this. Humanity has interpreted and reinterpreted their understanding of 'what is', since we were able to begin expressing things to each other in words. Each culture, each society, each country and each belief system, has owned concepts and interpreted things in their own way. And instead of these understandings bringing togetherness, they have brought separation and conflict, due to words and the interpretation of words. To bring humanity back together we need to strip away the words. When we strip away the words and feel *Truth*, and the resonance of *Truth*, we will all come together.

There is no need to define Truth, label Truth or own Truth.
Truth just 'Is'.

The clunky word-based understanding of 'Is', 'Am' and 'Me', written about in this book is for all people, of all faiths, and no faith.

It is for humanity, and we are all humans.

It is for each and every one of us, regardless of ALL things.

It can be placed alongside your belief system, within your belief system, or stand-alone with no belief system. It is the underpinning structure of all the above, or none of it. It really doesn't matter. It is for everyone to absorb as an individual. As I said, your interpretation will be according to your unique human experience, and your own unique soul. Your interpretation will be right for you, and your journey. It may differ from another's interpretation, but both will be right, if the Truth of what is said is *felt*, rather than *thought*.

We may all think it differently, but Truth is always the same.

So many wars have been fought over belief systems. There has been, and still is, so much pain, and so much suffering. There is still so much suppression due to ownership of beliefs, hierarchical structure, and man-made rules and complexities.

The words 'God', 'Soul' and 'Spirit' are so divisive and can cause so much conflict, even within oneself, that in some places in this book I have replaced them so that *Truth* can speak without causing disharmony. This is also so those with no belief, or who are vehemently anti-belief, can also connect to *Truth*, which tries to be heard within these pages.

It is for everyone, if they choose to listen.

And this listening is *always* a choice.

Therefore, I will seek to express the definition of certain words within the context of this book. This is not to cause offence, but purely to provide accessibility to all humans, of all faiths, and none. I meditated and awaited guidance, and these are the words which were presented.

'God'

God 'Is'.

God is a word which is understood and interpreted according to faith, or no-faith. It is a word which brings great comfort, or great conflict. God is defined in many ways and has many faces.

But the light (of God), which is the essence of *All*,
just 'Is'.
The essence of *All* cannot be described and cannot be interpreted,
it just 'Is'.

The word 'Is' can be preceded by your own word for God and can be followed by your own description of what you believe the qualities of your God/Gods/no-Gods to be.

*But essentially God cannot be defined, because God is indefinable,
and cannot be described, as it is infinitely creative and of infinite
possibility.*

God 'Is'.

To try to define that which 'Is', is futile. Therefore, when I use the words 'that which 'Is'', in the context of this book, I mean it to be that which is the love, light, essence and mystery of, and beyond, the label 'God'.

'Soul'

I 'Am' Soul

There are different interpretations and understanding of 'soul', and there are those who are uncomfortable with the word 'soul'.

We have been given various descriptions of what it is, what it means, and what its properties are. It has also been used as a weapon of fear. If you do this or that, this or that will happen to your soul. Fear is not acceptable.

The word 'soul' in the context of this book can be defined as your 'Am'. I *am* kind, I *am* tall, etc.... 'Am' can be preceded by 'I' (who you believe yourself to be) and can be followed by your own description of what you believe your qualities to be. To try to define the eternal essence of 'Am' within the infinite potential of your 'soul' is futile.

Your 'soul' cannot be defined, because 'soul' is indefinable,
and it cannot be described, as it is infinitely creative, and of infinite possibility.

I 'Am'.

When we sense and understand our essence of 'Am', which is soul, we find our peace and unconditional love. This is because our unique aspect of that which 'Is' sits within the centre of soul. This is our soul's connection to that which 'Is'.

In this book soul does not relate to any belief system or religious definition. Within these pages soul is the essence of our eternal 'Am'. Therefore, when I use the word 'soul', in the context of this book, I mean it to be your 'Am'; the multi-vibrational, multi-conscious, eternal 'Am' essence which is created around your unique facet of that which 'Is'.

It is the truth of us.

'Spirit-self'

Spirit-self – The incarnate facet of soul

In basic terms, soul separates an aspect of itself (spirit-self), which incarnates in this lifetime. Spirit-self, or separated aspect, always remains connected to, and part of, soul, via a cord of light.

When the spirit-self aspect of our soul incarnates into the physical, the *me* or *created-self* is formed around it.

I have found this easier to explain if we call our eternal 'Am' essence soul, and the incarnating facet of our soul, our spirit-self. Our spirit-self is that which our physical, emotional, and mind, 'me' forms around. It is an expression of the essence of part of our soul.

'Me'

Illusion of self (Created-self)

The word 'Me' is used to label the creation which is our human-self identity.

'Me' is not 'Am'.

Created-self is not the truth of our soul.

'Me', or who we perceive ourselves to be, is our manifestation of our created-self.

'Me' is created through our thoughts, emotions and physical circumstance. It is created through our upbringing, our conditioning, society, our social groups, our governments, the media and our belief systems.

Our created-self, or 'Me', is not our *Truth*. It is an illusion.

Me (Created-self) is built up around our spirit-self (the incarnate facet of soul).

Mel Cross

'Spiritual' or 'Spirit'

That which exists through and beyond the physical world, and is received not through our five senses, but is translated through our five senses. It is interpreted via our spirit-self by our mind, but understood within soul, or heart-space, where the gate to our soul is found.

It is a word which also means so many different things to so many different people and can create anxiety and anger in some individuals. Some people view the word within a religious context, but within this text it is standalone. It is a word for that which is beyond our tangible, physical, human experience, as a part of all faiths, and apart from all faiths.

'Spiritual' is a multi-level, multi-dimensional expression of 'Is', and flows with dynamic, creative 'Is'. It is created from 'Is' but is not corded to 'Is'.

'Heart-space'

There is a great deal spoken about heart-space within this book, as it is an essential gateway/level of vibration within us, through which we connect to our soul, our own Truth, and our own light - our unique aspect of the divine 'Is'.

In very basic terms, heart-space is the vibration of Love within our energy system. It connects to the vibration of love in all, and to the flowing love from that which 'Is'.

This is where our 'Am' essence - our soul, can be accessed, begins to be experienced, and where we start to understand our connection to everything.

The heart-space will be dealt with, in great depth, later within this book.

'Mind', or 'Mind-space'

Mind-space vibration is where we function within our head (mind), where we are within the illusion of our created-self ('me'), and where we believe ourselves to be separate from all things.

Our mind creates patterns of behaviour which minimise unnecessary physical, emotional or mental energy expenditure. We need to reach beyond these patterns for us to find our true way of being. Our true pattern.

The battle between consciously existing at the heart-space vibration, rather than existing within the mind-space vibration, is the one most hard to win.

Our mind is what stands at the gateway to our own truth, our soul.

'Energy'

Everything is made of energy/vibration. And everything from the physical, to that which 'Is', resonates at a certain frequency or level of vibration. Our soul and spirit-self are formed with energy and resonate at differing frequencies. I am not a scientist! This is the vocabulary I use to describe the indescribable, for our minds to try and grasp the idea in some way. As humans, if we cannot visualise it, we have trouble translating what is trying to be said into something tangible.

As everything is energy, everything is ultimately connected to, and part of, everything else. As spirit/created-self we exist as multiple single layers of vibration and our consciousness moves and flows freely within these energetic levels. This enables us to focus on one aspect of, or level of, energy at a time, enabling interpretation to take place within our human mind. We can influence and affect energy by focusing our consciousness.

When we operate as 'Am' essence soul, we can be.

This is when we energetically exist as a multi-vibrational soul-self, rather than multiple single levels of vibration as a spirit-self. Consciousness exists at all levels within soul simultaneously, without need of interpretation through mind.

Multi-level consciousness is wholeness of soul, and wholeness is peace. This is where 'Is'-ness is experienced, as we are whole and harmonious. But, as we are still operating within the confines of human, physical existence, this multi-level consciousness can focus on one level of vibration at a time, for our mind to be able to interpret what is experienced.

'No-thing'

The word 'no-thing', in the context of this work, means the space where there is an absence of a tangible *thing*, it is the space *between*. 'Nothing', on the other hand, implies an absence of all things. But, within this work, the word 'no-thing' sets to express the infinite potential of the emptiness from which all things come. It is not a space of nothing, it is the space of no-thing with the potential for the everything. It is the place from which all things come, and to which all things return. It is the place of infinite, flowing, dynamic, creative, that which 'Is'.

Words are so futile when trying to explain things which can only be felt or experienced. But we need to begin somewhere, to feed the mind, which in turn will keep it occupied so that true understanding can take place within the heart.

Everything seems so complex, and that is because it is, but it is also so utterly simple, and that is also because it is. There is a duality in this process and understanding; intangibly complex and blindingly simple. The separation of layers of energy, incarnation as spirit-self, and returning to and integration of soul, is frustratingly complex.

But existing as soul and wholeness is simple − it is just being.

All we need is love, faith, and trust, with surrender within stillness and humility. This will guide us to Truth.

And we need humour, lots of laughter, and hugs... also very important!

THE THREE PARTS OF 'IS'

Understanding the One

Words are so clumsy when describing that which needs explanation, but they are required to bring understanding to the mind, so I will do my best with them. In this chapter it is important to understand that the descriptions given are not statements of *fact*, they are statements of *possibility*. They are a way of giving the mind something visual and tangible to grasp, whilst true understanding will later be felt, deciphered, and understood within the heart-space, via soul, and your divine aspect of 'Is'.

I describe the three parts of 'Is' separately, so that we are able to grasp them, but ultimately they are manifestations of the same thing in different ways. They are three parts of the same whole.

Separate but together; three parts, but One.

The indescribable nature of infinite possibility wrapped within the purest nature of light and love. Yes – again it is futile, clunky, and utterly useless to try to explain using words.

The descriptions used are not in any way set to disrespect anyone's understanding of, or connection to, their own God/Gods/no God. They are purely to seek the core of what 'Is', and strip it back to its purity, simplicity and light. The overlaying of one's own belief, interpretation, scripture, or study, is entirely your choosing.

Everyone is unique, and your path to connection is your own.

The 'Is' above:
The constant emanator of love and light

The 'Is' that is pure peace, pure light and pure love, sits as the highest level of vibration.

It is, and always has been, radiating love, light and peace, in purest divine, formless, form.

It is the infinite vibration of love, and eternally emanates this love down through all levels of vibration, all dimensions, and all existence. It is eternal truth, of eternal forgiveness, ultimate harmony, and unbounded love, light and joy. This flowing love can be visualised as flowing white light.

The 'Is' above is – Love.

The 'Is' above, the constant emanator of love and light, eternally explores itself, via the unique facets of itself, receptive 'Is', the light which sits at the centre of each of our souls. These unique facets radiate infinite possibilities and combinations of colours to create unique multi-vibrational souls. These unique facets still contain the essence of 'Is' – Love.

The love which emanates from the 'Is' above, once truly experienced, will lead the individual to seek a more constant, more dynamic, more expanded relationship with 'Is', in deepest humility.

The 'Is' above, is the place our soul evolves towards, for it to integrate back to the place of its origin; to return our own unique aspect of the 'Is', back to the original 'Is'.

This is the emanating aspect of 'Is'.

The 'Is' through, around and in all things:
The dynamic, creative, flowing, no-thing

The 'Is' above, the constant emanator of love and light, separated to create light and dark. Dark is the absence of light. Absence is the 'no-thing'. The no-thing is where dynamic, creative 'Is' flows through, around and in all things. It is the space *between*.

It can be visualised as flowing darkness, and still contains the essence of 'Is' – Love.

Between, around, and through all atoms is the 'no-thing', which I sometimes refer to as being 'the grid', as this is how it has been shown to me. It is the space of infinite potential and infinite creativity. It is the space where everything comes from and goes back to. It is where the information of everything that was, is, and will be, is held. The eternal possibility of everything is in constant flow within the no-thing grid. It is divinely creative and infinitely informative. It is the space which holds and manifests the unique patterns of all things, bringing them in to form.

Where there is no-thing there is everything.

This is the dynamic aspect of 'Is'

The 'Is' within the soul:
The receptive aspect of 'Is'

The 'Is' light within the centre of each and every one of us gives life to our soul. It is a unique facet of that which 'Is' above.

This receptive aspect of 'Is' is found within soul via our heart-space. It is connected through each level of vibration, directly back to the highest vibrational aspect of 'Is' above; the constant emanator of love and light.

The connection between our unique receptive fragment of 'Is' and 'Is' above, is visualised as a cord of light. This cord of light is our cord of faith.

Within our heart-space we receive and sense the love from that which 'Is' above, via the cord of light into our unique receptive 'Is', at the centre of our soul. This pulsing, shining, utterly overwhelming, and totally humbling love, for which there are no words.

The soul can be visualised as a unique manifestation of all possibilities of colour, a unique pattern, with the flowing light of love into it from that which 'Is' above, and the flowing darkness through it from the dynamic, creative 'Is'.

The flowing darkness of *no-thing*, creative 'Is', flows patterns of possibility, which are sensed within the receptive aspect of 'Is'.

This is the receptive aspect of 'Is'.

It is important we try to visualise and understand the three aspects of 'Is' which create the Whole. Then we can begin to sense the differences of, and connect to, the three aspects of 'Is'.

The emanating white light of love, flowing with the dark eternal, dynamic creative potential of no-thing, weaving through the infinite colours of formless and form.

'Is' is through all, around all and in all. 'Is' is.

Once we understand the three, we will come to know the One.

Mel Cross

THE SEPARATION OF 'IS'

The building of patterns

Is' is.

'Is' always has been, and always will be.

'Is' began to explore infinite, creative, potential from the silence of love. It began to expand and separate love, to explore the infinite potential of 'Is'.

The One became the three, and the three remained the One.

The 'Is' above remained the constant emanator of love and light (Creator).

The 'Is' through, around, and in all things, became the dynamic, creative, flowing no-thing (Creative).

The 'Is' above, the divine emanator of love and light, began to create unique aspects of itself, which became, and still become, the light within our souls; the receptive aspect of 'Is' within soul (the Creation).

'Is' separated the vibration of pure frequency, and created a vibration of three,
in perfect harmony.

To bring the pure frequency of 'Is' into the physical, it had to separate itself still further. The vibration of purity separated and separated, and became lower and lower, until it brought itself into physical form.

It is like a diamond separating the colours contained within a white light. The light begins white and is separated into colours (or frequencies/vibrations), each colour containing different properties, but each harmonious with the whole.

For the sake of simplicity, we shall call the 'Is' vibration above, white, bringing the vibrations down through the rainbow of colours to red; the physical vibration. All held by the no-thing (absence of colour). So, white, violet, indigo, blue, green, yellow, orange, red. To say this is simplistic is the greatest of understatements!

Each level of vibration/frequency between the pure 'Is' above, and physical reality as we observe it, contains immeasurable multiple layers of vibration. As each layer comes down from 'Is' it is of a certain frequency and contains general characteristics of that frequency. All that exists in a spiritual dimension, at that frequency, contains similar characteristics. Each is harmonious to the other at the same frequency.

Each layer of frequency contains infinite fragments of frequency of the same vibration. At the centre of each fragment of frequency is one single dot of divine white light.

Imagine a sea of red beads as the sea of red frequency all vibrating the same, and each of these beads has one dot of white light at the centre of it. Each bead has light, has been created by light, but is not corded to light.

The sea of all beads (or frequencies) are the building blocks of creation. They can be pulled together to create infinite possibilities of patterns by the dynamic, creative no-thing 'Is'.

This fundamental separation of vibration underpins and weaves through many beliefs and is explained and expressed in many ways.

Each at an accessible level of comprehension and understanding at the time each belief system was conceived, illuminated and shared.

All different, all the same, all divinely beautiful.

As we are all unique facets of the divine Truth, so too all belief systems are unique facets of the divine Truth.

All of this should be harmonious, not discordant. It is our human condition which creates this disharmony, not the beliefs themselves. When we view things from the three lower levels of vibration, physical, emotional, and mind, as humans do at present, we only see the separation and difference. When we can raise our vibration to the frequency of 'love', or 'heart-space', we will only see the similarity, unity and wholeness of the perceived separated parts.

There are infinite possibilities of creation, and there are infinite possibilities of beliefs, which have been formed to explain what 'Is' to the mind. When we operate as heart-space humans, at a frequency of love, we no longer need explanation to the mind as we feel the Truth within our hearts. Beliefs are a manmade structure in which to explore the Truth. They have grown up around incredible, insightful, Is-being individuals, concepts and ideas, each expressing the 'Is' in a unique and beautiful way.

It is right that these beliefs are different as they create growth, exploration, contemplation, creation and expansion. But these should be explored in harmony, as they are all expressions of 'Is', in order to create the Whole.

Everything written about is in the expansion of exploration,
and contraction of togetherness,
and harmony applies to all things.

The Butterfly

Our role is to be a beacon,
a light,
a voice,
a mouth-piece of Truth.
To speak the Truth.
To be the Truth.

It is not complicated.
But we as humans have made it complicated.

It is like capturing the butterfly, and dissecting it cell
        by cell, piece by piece.
Would we categorise these pieces?
Price them?
Separate them?
Would we fight over the pieces?
Would we claim some as more important, more
        beautiful, or of more worth than others?
Would we put each wing, each leg, each piece, in
        separate cases and claim we had the only
        piece that mattered?
Would we worship the leg and forget the butterfly?

Our fighting, our greed, our need to categorise,
to own,
to rank ourselves according to who we think we are,
or what we materially own,

washes away all reason.

We push away our soul, and the Truth of what Is,

so that these become so, so far away from us that we
no longer know them.

We have forgotten the incandescent beauty of the
LIVING butterfly;

its worth as a Whole,

its magnificent radiance,

its exquisite beauty.

We have forgotten that together it is alive,

it breathes,

it flies,

it IS.

The Truth is like the butterfly.

If it is not Whole, it does not live.

We do not take it apart.

We do not separate its pieces.

We do not own it.

We do not claim it at the exclusion of others.

We do not cage it with our greed,

and we do not dull its nature by forcing upon it our
mind-produced human idea of what it
should be.

We let it be,

let it live,

let it fly,
and celebrate it.
We draw the beauty of all that it is deep into our soul,
        and let it unfurl our own wings and our own
        beauty.
We let it enter us and let us become the butterfly also.

We will all soar together,
Colourful, vibrant, beautiful, joyous and utterly alive.
We will fly to different places, in different ways,
to share the understanding of the butterfly,
with different colours and in different tongues.
No way better than another.
No judgement.
Just beauty and freedom by example.

Not by dictation of old ideals, old standards, old ways.
For there is no place for these now.
These have been rotten and stagnant and infectious
        for too long.
This has to end,
and end it will.

We will find our voices,
spread our wings,
and show the only way is in the wholeness of the
        butterfly;
And that wholeness,
and that way is

IS-BEING

Love...

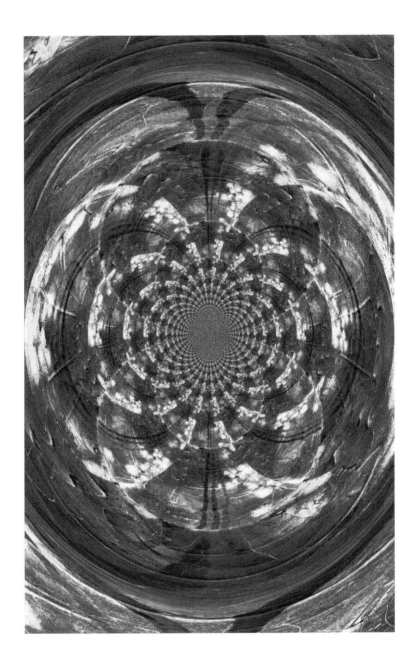

THE SEPARATION OF 'IS' INTO 'AM'

Creation of the soul

The 'Is' above separated into layers of vibrational existence, all emanating from pure 'Is' love and light, with all things returning to pure 'Is', love and light.

The 'Is' created the layers of vibration to create difference.
Difference causes exploration, expression and creation.
'Is' created separation of itself, but always remaining, at source, pure vibration.

This separation of 'Is' is also reflected in the creation of 'Am's (Souls).

'Is' separates a unique facet of itself.
This unique facet of itself stays 'pure' in love and light.
It stays corded to source but is brought down through the layers of vibration towards physical. Each layer of vibration it is brought down through, creates a separation of part of that frequency, to begin building and creating a unique soul around the fragment.

So, soul connects to each level of vibration and has each frequency of vibration moving freely within itself, all together, all at the same time, harmoniously.

Soul contains all vibrations in varying unique amounts simultaneously but connects to each separate level of vibration created by 'Is', via the cord connecting to 'Is' above, the highest pure vibration. When soul reaches love frequency of vibration it stops descending the frequencies, as soul does not fully incarnate into physical form.

'Is' separates a unique divine facet of itself to create soul, and soul separates a divine facet of itself (spirit-self), to incarnate into physical form.

Soul and spirit-self stay connected via the cord of 'Is' that runs from the divine source of 'Is' above, into the centre of soul, and down into the centre of spirit-self.

Soul exists as a multi-vibrational, free-flowing, multi-conscious, energetic form, with the light of that which 'Is' at the centre of it. The higher frequency vibrations are closer to the centre, radiating out to the lower frequencies towards the outer layers of soul, but all free-flowing.

For soul to pull down an aspect of itself to create spirit-self, it needs to vibrationally separate still further to explore, create and express in a physical form.

Therefore, the aspect which creates spirit-self splits part of its multi-vibrational form and pulls it into a more distinctly single-layered form. Each vibration of spirit-self is a separate layer of frequency, emanating out from the small light of that which 'Is' at the centre of spirit-self. There are several reasons for this.

The first three levels of vibration, physical, emotional, and mind are only created when incarnating as spirit-self into physical form. They do not exist within soul. These low-level vibrations are discordant to soul and cause disharmony to it. They are the layers which soul must communicate through, to bring attention to itself, and what it is trying to express.

The physical, emotional and mind layers are the ones which hold our 'me' (created-self) information, and where disharmonious experiences are held as coagulated energy, ready for us to address and dissolve. When we pass over from this life, these three levels of vibration are dropped and dissolve. Any significant, unresolved, coagulated energy at these three levels, which does not dissolve, drop, or get removed by that which 'Is' through love at the time of passing, collect on the outer layer of soul, to be harmonised when we next incarnate. These coagulations return with us when we next incarnate, for us to address and dissolve. The disharmony caused to soul, when low-level coagulations affect it, is traumatic. We do not want this disharmony to be with us after we pass.

We are at peace when our spirit-self integrates with soul when passing, without discordant low-level coagulations, in complete harmony.

For soul to experience the pain and disharmony created, when we live as spirit-self in human form, would be unimaginable. Therefore, pain and disharmony are only experienced within the incarnate spirit-self aspect of soul, but the non-incarnated soul (Am) remains harmonious, receiving only the information from incarnate experience, but not the experiences themselves.

This is one of the reasons why spirit-self and soul are connected and in communication, but soul is kept separate and protected, with its access point being within the vibration of 'heart-space' and 'love'.

Another reason for the separation is that the enormity and potential of soul could cause major issues, if being disharmoniously driven by mind or emotion. Soul potential must only be accessed in love, faith, trust, truth, surrender, stillness and humility. This keeps soul and the 'Is' within soul, safe. As humans, we 'think' we know best, but soul understands that we don't! Therefore, soul can send down information to human, but physical human cannot force its will on to soul. Unfortunately, physical human can force its will onto spirit-self, and this is where the disharmony and pain begin. This is also where our learning, growth and understanding begin.

The separation of layers of energy, when we incarnate as spirit-self, is also so that we can connect to them individually and experience them separately. We need to experience them individually, and separately, so that we can learn, explore and express our unique aspect of soul, our spirit-self incarnated. Separation, as said earlier, is so that the differences between the experiences can be felt and assimilated, and so learning and understanding can take place. Difference creates comparison, and difference creates growth.

The movement of consciousness between different layers of vibration and experience can be tremendously fast and utterly fluid, but the vibrational layers are still experienced and focussed on one at a time, as this is how our consciousness works in a human form at present.

As a human being, with a human brain, we have a VERY limited capacity for receiving and translating information. Our brains, at present, as an incarnate fragment of soul, can only consciously interpret one level of vibrational information at a time, and even this is very limited. Enormous tracts of information are missed because we cannot receive, process, and interpret them, consciously. This constant stream of information though, is received, processed and interpreted by soul, to and via the spirit-self. We are not conscious of this. Our conscious focus, when we live as incarnate spirit-self, is usually focussed on more tangible single level frequencies. Usually physical, emotional and mind level frequencies, as these are the layers which are closest to us as physical beings.

When we incarnate our soul we can receive, process, and interpret, all information by *being*, and sitting within the flow of all that 'Is', as multi-vibrational consciousness. Within soul this infinite amount of information is worked with, then unique patterns, connections and relevant information are passed to the brain.

When we function as incarnate spirit-self, we interpret information through our senses, to our brain, to our spirit-self, to our soul. Spirit-self and soul are always collecting and passing information to each other through their connection at heart-space, which sometimes reaches our mind, via spirit-self, as 'creative' insight and inspiration.

All of this will be dealt with in later chapters, but for now we need to understand we exist as separate layers of energy as a spirit-self incarnate, because we only require physical, emotional and mind layers when we incarnate, which are dropped as we pass over and integrate back into soul. Separation of layers creates difference, and difference creates opportunity for learning.

SOUL AND SPIRIT-SELF

The differences between them

When we are born, we incarnate as a unique facet of soul (our true-self) within a physical body. That unique facet (which I refer to as our 'spirit-self') is pure and is also aware that it is an aspect of soul. When we incarnate into physical form, the three lower levels of energetic vibration are created within our energy system. These three lower levels of vibration are situated closest to our physical body within our energy system. These are the physical, emotional, and mind layers. They contain information concerning the physical, emotional and mental personality (created-self); the 'me', in this lifetime.

The three lower levels of vibration formed when we become physical, may contain any aspects of previous energetic coagulation which were not harmonised, removed, or dissolved, at our time of passing from a previous incarnation. If they are still present on the outer layer of soul when we incarnate, we bring these coagulations into this lifetime to resolve and dissolve. We cannot incarnate at a higher level of soul evolution if we contain aspects of coagulated energy of a lower frequency. Therefore, we incarnate as more of an embodiment of the coagulated energies from the previous spirit-self, which we need to then address. This is due to the attraction of similar fragments from the layers we descend through when re-incarnating. Like attracts like, therefore we may incarnate with an exaggerated form of coagulation to draw attention to it.

This is a process of harmonisation. This is NOT a form of judgement. It does not make us *lesser*. It is a learning experience required by soul, for it to return to harmony.

Journeys are <u>NOT</u> judgements.

So, when we are born, we are a pure spirit-self (incarnate facet of soul), with body, plus undissolved energy from previous incarnations.

Also, within the womb, when our physical body is being formed, energetic genetic memory (energy patterns) from parents or ancestors are passed on to us. This is reinforced, once born, by the programming passed to us by the behaviours of our parents. This reinforcing causes the energetic genetic memory to be coagulated into the individual's energy system, thus reinforcing and passing on the energetic predisposition in a physical/emotion/mind way.

But it does not have to be like this.

This parental, or ancestral, memory/resonance can be harmonised and dissolved, as with all energetic disharmony. The coagulation formed, when energetic genetic memory is reinforced by parental behaviours and vibrations, requires more effort to be dissolved, as they are multi-faceted coagulations. They are also held in place by energetic cording (from one person to another), which also needs to be resolved and dissolved to harmonise the coagulation. The spirit-self therefore, when incarnating into human form may already contain some form of disharmony which will need dissolving. These disharmonies are held in the three lower levels of vibration; the physical, emotional and mind layers.

Between the third and fourth layers of vibration (the 'mind' and the 'heart-space'), a constriction in our connection between our soul and our incarnating spirit-self is created. This restriction is created by, and because of, the formation of the lower-level physical, emotional, and mind levels of vibration. This is the formation of our 'me', our 'created-self'. The restriction is created this way so that the disharmonies of living within the human experience do not affect or contaminate soul. But it is this constriction which also keeps us from being able to see beyond these layers, to recognise our true soul nature, and that which 'Is'. It has been designed this way, as the levels of vibration in soul, resonating at heart-space and above, are pulled out from the incarnating light of 'Is' at the centre of our soul. Soul is created by the separation of vibration from the incarnating receptive aspect of 'Is'.

The three layers of physical, emotional and mind, which form around the descending facet of soul (spirit-self), to create our 'me', are drawn to the incarnating spirit-self from the three external layers of vibration as spirit-self descends into the physical. They form according to our spirit-self blue-print in our soul along with creative that which 'Is'. These three layers are from that which 'Is' but are not corded to that which 'Is'. They are not part of soul but are required to be part of the incarnating spirit-self for it to become physical, created-self, 'me'. Therefore, these lower-levels dissolve when spirit-self passes back into soul. They are transient vibrations required for the physical formation of the human body in physical form.

At present we believe that we are beneath the light of our soul (our 'higher-self'), and beneath that which 'Is', because we so often only live our human lives within our physical, emotional and mind layers of existence. We feel trapped within our 'me'.

But this is an illusion.

We believe that this illusion cannot be pushed through to reach the Truth of our soul, and the light and love of that which 'Is'.

We believe that we are below and beneath that which 'Is', and that we can only *glimpse* at the true, pure, light of our soul.

Society, religion, media, social groups, ethnicity, cultural surroundings, class etc. are all man-made structures which categorise, subjugate, subdue, shackle and create hierarchy. These man-made structures create energetic debris at a physical, emotional and mind level. These structures cause us to move further and further from our true soul nature, and that which 'Is'. They cause us to become more encased within our 'me'; our created identity around our incarnate spirit-self.

These structures, if we allow them, keep us from our spiritual evolution, and keep us from incarnating our own true soul and our own unique, divine, aspect of 'Is'.

These structures have been built to create power-centric hierarchy which can subdue and imprison our true soul nature. The wisdom and beauty of our true soul nature is challenging to these structures.

Soul cannot be subdued, intimidated, or lied to.

Soul resonates at a frequency of love, light, and truth.

Soul will not tolerate the discomfort and illusion created by these lower-level vibrations. These structures create a judgemental society, where personal questioning leads to hurt feelings, insecurity and fear. They intimidate, categorise and dictate. They try to place us into boxes to create hierarchy. But as unique manifestations of that which 'Is', we are all different.

There is no 'one size fits all'.

Of course, we have similarities, but essentially, we are unique. It is this unique divine aspect of that which 'Is', our soul, which we are here to explore, express and evolve. When we are not able to feel and express our true soul-self, this creates discomfort and disharmony within our energetic system. This disharmony and discomfort causes sadness, fear and a sense of something missing, loss or lack. These feelings are the result of our soul trying to communicate with us. These discordant experiences, if not addressed, then create coagulations of energy which move us further and further away from true soul recognition and incarnation.

With the formation of discordant societal structures, in all shapes and guises, we are always disharmonious, as we never truly *fit* into any category. We are lucky if we find a category of *best fit* from which to operate. This is also exacerbated by our social media influenced culture. We are bombarded with unobtainable images and created *ideals*. We are terrified that we do not fit, that we do not align with the images and that we do not demonstrate these ideals. We deeply fear *not fitting in*.

These societal structures which keep us bound by fear are often motivated by power and money. Power and money are 'mind' vibration, and fear affects our physical, emotional and mind levels of vibration, all of which keep us blind within our low level 'me' – our created-self.

When we operate in low level 'me' vibration we believe we are alone and are out for ourselves only. This 'me' attitude causes us to fight and to try to rank ourselves alongside others. We do not view the 'bigger picture'. We do not understand our interconnectivity or the outcomes of our selfishness. We do not consider the effects of our actions, our behaviours or our thoughts on others.

We only see *me* and rarely view *we*.

When we live in the state of 'me', at lower levels of vibration, blind to our true soul nature, we hurt each other, we lie, we are selfish, egotistical, and we may display many other unpleasant human aspects and behaviours. We are distracted by physical existence, both pain and pleasure, by our emotional experience, and by all aspects of our mind and thoughts. They are also the levels at which malevolent aspects of spiritual manifestation can influence, distract and cause disharmony.

This is the playground of the malevolent.

These manifestations of spiritual energy do not want us to access our higher vibrations and true soul-self, so they create havoc in the illusion of 'me'. This is where our energetic system can be manipulated and affected to keep us vibrating at lower frequencies. It keeps us from evolving and therefore sensing clearly and exposing that which does not operate from a point of love and truth. These distractions and causes of coagulation and disharmonious energy can also cause us to behave and react in less than positive ways. These less than positive ways are at odds with our soul. This causes further discomfort and disharmony.

Thus 'me' (created-self) and 'soul' (true-self) conflict can manifest in physical, emotional, and mind ways, to bring attention to something which needs resolving practically, and requires dissolving energetically.

This resolving and dissolving needs to be done at many levels.

Something which is disharmonious needs to be addressed at a physical level. How can we change our physical body, surroundings, or

47

situation, to cause no, or less, discomfort? How can we resolve or create peace within our emotional system? How can we retrain our mind/brain/behaviours so that we behave differently, and how can we create new reactions and behaviours which are more harmonious? Once we have addressed issues at these three practical levels, how can we identify, resolve, and dissolve any energetic coagulation and disharmony within our energetic system?

Addressing things at a practical level removes the causes of the disharmony. Removal of the coagulated energy stops the repetition of the disharmonious action and clears it. We repeat disharmonious actions to draw attention to an issue in our energetic system if we have not cleared it. The disharmonious coagulation attracts similar vibrations to it which causes repetition of discordant circumstances and patterns of behaviour. Thus, clearing both practically and energetically creates space and clarity, and prevents repetition.

Within this space and clarity, we begin to catch glimpses of our true soul-nature. Our consciousness begins to sense and be able to communicate our *something more*; our *Truth*. It is only when we begin to penetrate, dissolve, and reach up through the levels of vibration, that we begin to see, sense, understand and connect to, our true nature; our soul. When we begin to penetrate these layers toward the light we sense above and inside ourselves, we begin to sense peace, love and light. The more of our created 'me' we dissolve, both behaviourally and energetically, the more of our soul we uncover, and the more of our 'Is'-essence we sense. This, in turn, begins to raise our vibration, as we are no longer burdened with the weight of the coagulations, which were holding us down in lower layers. As our vibration begins to raise towards existence at heart-space level, where the door to our soul sits, we begin to understand an existence of peace, love and light. We begin to understand our interconnected nature, and know the *we*, instead of the *me*.

Our conscious gaze can move between all levels of energetic existence all of the time. This is how we are able to have creative revelation, spiritual experience, flashes of peace and love, moments of clarity, and sense our 'Is' connection. Sometimes this is experienced when meditating or in contemplation, as we have entered the heart-space level of vibration, and within this vibration we can sense the soul. Meditation and contemplation remove physical, emotional, and mind distractions so we can consciously connect to heart-space, soul, and that which 'Is'. But this state is temporary, as we enter meditation or contemplation and then leave this state, therefore leaving the heart-space vibration.

What we must strive towards is creating this state permanently, whilst in physical existence. The reason these moments are fleeting, and not sustained, is because we are existing as 'me' within the lower three layers of vibration and are only *visiting* heart-space vibration. Once we have worked on ourselves practically, within the mind, the emotions, and the physical, and dissolved disharmonious vibrations caused by experiences within these aspects/levels of 'me', our vibration is no longer held at 'me' level. This is when we begin to raise into heart-space vibration in a more consistent and permanent way. This is the vibration of love, peace and healing.

At this level we recognise the 'door to our soul' and begin to sense our unique aspect of that which 'Is', which sits at the very centre of our soul.

It is at this point that we may begin to experience the very distinct separation of 'me' (created-self) and 'am' (soul-self). We begin to identify and recognise the difference. We begin to sense the harmony, peace, love, light and beauty within our soul. This brings great emotion and relief. We are beginning to recognise *home*.

When we work at existing within our heart-space frequency, we begin to resonate with Love. Instead of seeking 'energetic feeding' from external sources, and external validation, we begin to recognise and understand that this is no longer necessary or valid, as we are in constant flow of love and light from that which 'Is'. We recognise our Truth, our unique essence of the divine, and know it contains its own perfection and beauty. There is no disharmony in this; nothing is at odds with anything else. It no longer matters where we sit in the scheme of things, where we fit, or where we are accepted, as our soul is perfect.

The soul sits in peace, it fits with all, and it accepts itself in its entirety.
It just is.
Perfection, stillness and beauty.

When we touch our soul, we want to remain within it and retain this feeling. So, working at dissolving lower disharmonious energies enables our consciousness more fluidity and movement between these lower frequency layers, therefore allowing more freedom to move into heart-space frequency.

The dissolving of the three lower levels of frequency dissolves your 'me' – your created identity.

The dissolving of created identity causes the expansion of heart-space frequency within your energetic system.

As heart-space frequency expands, the constriction between spirit-self and soul lessens and conscious communication between them increases. When our spirit-self consciousness moves into heart-space, it begins to connect through the heart-space vibration with soul. This connection, and the expansion of heart-space due to the energetic dissolving of the lower levels, is what enables soul to be pulled down into this physical incarnation.

Our spirit-self (the unique facet of our soul), which sits within our created identity in this lifetime, is no longer required in the same separated sense, as we are sensing and beginning to function within our truth, rather than our created false truth. Therefore, with conscious dedication, we can facilitate the merging back of spirit-self with soul-self and can begin to live as soul-self in this lifetime.

We can do this as we no longer need to retain the created 'me' spirit-self incarnation as a mediator between soul and mind (created-self). Disharmonious energy, energetic cords which held us in place, behaviours, thoughts, and physical circumstance from our 'me' are no longer relevant.

We can begin to become our Truth and seek to exist as our true soul nature.

This is instant cleansing and harmonising in this current lifetime. We no longer must wait until the time at which we pass over for this to take place. We can practically assist in bringing harmony to our own soul. That which we harmonise within this lifetime will not be carried forward into further lifetimes.

When we bring our true soul vibration into this existence, it resonates at a frequency of unconditional love, healing, light, and the interconnected nature of all things. Soul emanates these qualities always and affects the frequencies of all those around it. Just by being soul-self you are raising the vibration of all. The soul-self frequency will awaken the heart-space within others. Therefore, by radiating our soul frequency, the vibration of the people we connect with will raise, and this will ripple out to others. This will continue, on and on, until a full vibrational shift to heart-space living takes place.

Even if we do not incarnate our soul but can consciously exist within the frequency of love at heart-space, as our spirit-self, we will help to raise the frequencies of others, which will awaken them to their own heart-space and love vibration. The planetary frequencies are already changing to heart-space frequency to accommodate the shift. This will ensure an environment which is more comfortable for heart-space humans and soul-self humans to exist, and less comfortable for those existing as 'me' in lower-level frequencies.

Once this shift has taken place we will work as unique aspects of divine incarnation, but collectively as One. The oneness, or box that we all inhabit, will be one celebrating and supporting the All. We will recognise, at the centre of each of us, the aspect of the same or One. The 'Is' vibration. We will not be able to lie, to hurt, to cheat, or to be selfish, as our core is core.

If we hurt one, we hurt all. If we love one, we love all.

This is the most important thing to remember. When we work on ourselves, we work on the 'All'. By making ourselves the purest vessel of love, light and peace, we are creating love, light and peace for All.

This is not selfish; this is self-less.

The journey to soul-self existence in this lifetime is hard, challenging, and often incredibly painful. It challenges us physically, emotionally, mentally and spiritually. It exposes experiences we've buried deeply within us, and causes us to identify aspects of ourselves, and our identity, which we would rather not acknowledge or reveal. But this is necessary for us to address our lives, change ourselves ('me'), and dissolve any discordant energy or blockages. Sometimes this dissolving happens by itself through changes in life, changes to 'me', or through circumstances. Sometimes it is dissolved through positive actions, behaviours, or thoughts. Sometimes it is dissolved by that which 'Is'. Sometimes, when we are so disharmonious and encased in calcified energy, we break, either physically, emotionally, mentally or spiritually. This breakage causes cracking and dissolving of calcified energy for us to glimpse our soul and our Truth, for us to escape destruction.

We can ask members of our religious or spiritual communities to help us dissolve our disharmony. And, through positive thinking, prayer, their skills/teachings, and the love and light of that which 'Is' working through them, they may be able to facilitate this.

Also, genuine healing modalities can assist in dissolving discordant/calcified energy.

But, unless we remove the physical/emotional/mental vibration, energetic cords, behaviours, and circumstances, which produced the discordancy in the first place, we will only reform the same blockages.

Some say that it is up to 'Is' alone to cleanse us, purify us, and remove and forgive our disharmonies. But it is our responsibility to work with this too. We are moving from passive acceptance to dynamic action. We are responsible for our own energetic system. And, at the heart of this system, is our soul and our own unique aspect of that which 'Is'. We say our body is a temple, and indeed it is, as our energetic system is the home of our light. Our bodies are quite literally our temples of light. Therefore, we should work at removing all bricks, blocks, and walls in order to resonate and shine as the pure light that we are.

We work with the light, within the light and are part of the light...

Mel Cross

EVOLUTION OF HUMANS AND EVOLUTION OF BELIEFS

The past and the present

As I now begin to talk about beliefs, I am aware I may cause ripples of discomfort. This discomfort is not to cause distress, it is to point towards and resolve that which needs addressing, within those who feel it ripple.

All beliefs and all faiths are indeed a beautiful thing. Each one is a manifestation of that which 'Is', in different ways, different structures, different faces, different explanations. All of them created in separation for exploration and growth, and for learning and expansion. Each belief containing aspects of divine Truth, divine learning, and divine exploration.

We all have so much to learn from each other, if we just shared and listened, rather than claiming exclusive ownership and regurgitating hollow dictation.

Each belief exploring the same aspects and different aspects, but each one of them containing some of the *Truth*. These differences were created for comparison, creativity, exploration and understanding.

It is only through difference that growth and change take place.

This vital element has been forgotten. All beliefs have the element of divine Truth at their core or explore and express different elements of that divine Truth.

Please forgive my lack of detail, and lack of knowledge, regarding belief systems. My understanding of these has come through information I have absorbed along my journey and has not been intimately researched or learned. It is important, as I have said, that what I write comes from the purity of guided direction from the source of that which 'Is', rather than contained within the structures of belief systems. It is important to bring the purity of this instruction, without structure, so that it can be placed within, alongside, or apart from, beliefs. Therefore, in some places, it may appear naïve, uninformed, unresearched or lacking. But that is deliberately so, not due to my ego believing my way is 'right', for I have no ego in the traditional sense. It is not because I don't believe I need to intimately know each belief, because I would love to wrap around what I say the security of that which has come before. This would be so much more comfortable for me! But, if I try to fit my understanding into what has gone before, then I negate its purity and its Truth.

If you read the whole book and say you know it all already, that is good. It means you have found good instruction or have listened to that which you were given. But remember to work at embodying what you 'know' rather than storing it as a trophy within the mind. If you read it and say, 'this has all been done before', within a belief in which you are familiar, this is good. It means you have identified the divine Truth within the belief. Feel free to add your meat to the bones of what is here from your previous learning, in any way you are comfortable, or that brings clarity and understanding to you.

This book is fluid, flowing, and in the constant process of learning and unlearning.
Read it, share it, split it, turn it upside down and inside out.
Let it create discussion, let it shake, and let it soothe.
It is what it is...take it and use it as you will.
You can take what I say, or not, it does not matter.
For that which I am given I must share, and it is for you to embrace, or not.

Everything is always a choice.
And choice is a precious gift.

If it makes you cross, this is also good, it means it is flagging up a discordant strand within you which needs to be identified and harmonised. If it makes you think, or change one tiny thing, this is movement, and movement is good. Movement means you are working with the *flow*, and *flow* is the dynamic, creative aspect of that which 'Is'.

If it contrasts wildly with your beliefs, this is also good. This highlights contrast, contrast brings contemplation and exploration, and this in turn promotes growth.

So, it is through purity not ignorance, trust and not ego, that I write in simplicity and with lack of underpinning research. It is not from lack of respect, but it is from total respect of, and faith in, the understanding given in love and purity to me. Also, words are inadequate, and rules are restrictive for that which needs expression, so it is given in simplicity for you to place within your own context.

As human beings began to have an awareness of that which 'Is', this awareness was worshipped and expressed within the context in which we lived. It was about the elements, the animals, the seasons, the sun and moon, the plants, the miracle of reproduction and our connection to our ancestors. The 'Is' was understood in the context of survival. Survival and ancestral memory are held within the first layer of the energetic field. The world existed at a more physical level; therefore, our conscious attention was more often within the physical layer of our energetic system. Because of the uncomplicated nature of basic survival living, man was more connected to the spiritual realms. There was less emotional and intellectual clutter to get in the way.

Humans were more harmonious with that which 'Is,' due to the simplicity of life, and their fluid connection to the natural world in which they lived and expressed themselves. They were connected to, and in communication with, nature, the dynamic, flowing, 'Is', and with spiritual dimensions.

As human societies changed, Gods and beliefs evolved, from physical expressions of that which 'Is', through emotional expressions of that which 'Is', and on into Gods and beliefs of knowledge, wisdom and intellect, or 'mind' expressions of that which 'Is'.

We began with our physical nature, then emotional, and then our intellect and mind, both in practical existence and within our belief systems. This evolution is also reflected in the evolution of the human brain; from survival, to emotional, to reasoning and intellect. Each of these evolutions reflects the other. Each of equal value, and each containing understanding and underpinning truths for that which was to be built upon them.

Humanity has evolved and explored through the lower levels of vibration, and now continues onwards as we evolve spiritually, and raise our consciousness to higher and higher levels and understanding.

These earlier beliefs were easier to grasp as they were all expressions of the lower three levels of vibration; the physical, the emotional and the mind. They were expressions of our exploration of what it is to be human, they were expressions of our created-self, our 'me'. This we could grasp. We could identify with these beliefs and Gods as we recognised their attributes within ourselves and within our lives. These Gods and beliefs were extreme expressions of human attributes. We could explore and understand ourselves through our beliefs. They were expressions of that which 'Is', within the three lower levels of vibration. When I say lower levels, this is not a judgement, and this is not giving them less value. It is purely that they are energetically denser and vibrating at a lower frequency. They are the layers which are denser and closer to our physical being. They are the layers which are created when we physically manifest within this lifetime, which are not present when we exist purely as our soul-self.

Then the ways of love and peace were brought to us through incredible and most holy individuals. This is when the way of love, light, harmony, and peace were taught. Through love, faith, trust, truth, surrender, stillness and humility we have tried to understand and embody this way of love.

These ideals have been the hardest to grasp, and even harder to live.

As human beings, our light is clouded by the physical, emotional and mind levels of existence. We have found this next stage of spiritual evolution so very hard to put in place. This is because we are moving from a created-self set of belief systems, to a soul-self set of belief systems. We are moving from our physical self to our spiritual self, and this requires a great leap of faith and understanding.

The structures of beliefs based on love and peace, have been set in place to give a mind-based framework for a love-based concept to be explored. But it is a tricky one. Because the mind-based structure is what keeps us from fully embracing the love-based way of existence. But the love-based way of existence is so very hard to stay focussed on, without the mind being engaged and occupied. The individual, until current times, has required the structure of beliefs to have the security of exploration of self and that which 'Is'. But the change in emphasis is now taking place, and change is most definitely taking place.

Humankind is now moving on to the next stage of spiritual evolution, and it is being felt in every belief system, and by those with no belief system. The shift is monumental. We are entering the stage of Divine Communication via the vibration/level of Love. We must exist at the frequency of Love, which was brought and taught by previous inspirational and holy individuals, to bring about the next stage of spiritual evolution, that of Divine Communication. We are shifting from

'Passive Receivers' as incarnate spirit-self, to 'Dynamic Creators', from the position of incarnate soul.

When we exist at the frequency of Love, we experience greater connection to that which 'Is', and interconnectivity to all other beings. Therefore, when truly living at Love vibration, or what I refer to as 'heart-space' vibration, we no longer require the belief systems as structures in which to connect to the divine, as we are connected to the divine within, and our spiritual community is every single living being on the planet.

Our 'Is' is within every belief, and no belief.
Our spiritual community is every living thing.

We respect each belief structure as a unique manifestation of the divine, just as each of us is a unique manifestation of the divine. We are happy in the company of all, and we are happy within the beliefs of all. Everything is a manifestation and expression of that which 'Is'. And Love is the cord, which connects all that is, together.

The vibration of the planet has raised to accommodate this spiritual evolution. It is now vibrating at the frequency of Love. This frequency is of great comfort for those existing in heart-space, but wholly uncomfortable for those unconsciously wandering in the physical, emotional, and mind vibrations.

People are awakening to their spiritual natures, to their divine connection, and to their love of, and interconnectivity to, all. They are doing this within belief systems, and despite belief systems. They are excited and scared in equal measure. They are seeking to find answers, teachers, and places to learn, and this is a crucial and critical time. Individuals are seeking answers in the wrong places, and from the wrong teachers. Wrong, in this instance, is not a judgement, 'wrong' in this instance, means that which is not appropriate for the support, nurturing and growth of the evolving individual. Yes, there is a great deal to be learned from every wrong turn in life, and, in fact, it is from mistakes which we tend to learn the most. But when we are seeking guidance it is much easier to find it from those who have been given the syllabus!

What is happening is that these 'awakened' individuals are seeking guidance from those spiritual workers who sometimes are working with old structures, with old understanding, and (though they would never admit it or recognise it) from their ego. They have wrapped their whole identity around their chosen way of working and will not release this grip. This grip is caused by lack of trust, lack of faith and lack of understanding. When we believe there is only one way, and it is the right way, whether in beliefs or spiritual systems, we are working from mind and emotion. This will not bring about spiritual growth and evolution. We must remember and remember well – spiritual experience is a side-effect of walking the path of spiritual evolution. To identify yourself with the experience is to pull yourself from the very path which led you to the experience! It is complex and yet simple, and as with all, there are opposing dynamics.

Therefore, we need to walk the path of evolution with love, faith, trust, truth, surrender, stillness and humility. We must walk it alone, as each path is unique. But all paths lead eventually to soul-integration. The bringing of total peace, pure love, multi-conscious, multi-vibrational, multi-connected, divine communion, into the physical.

So, where do we go?

Our faiths need to learn and support this evolution, our energy workers/spiritual teachers need to learn and support this evolution, our medical professions and those who work with the mind need to understand the process, and the importance of what is happening, and learn about and support this evolution. This evolution is happening, and at present it is chaotic and disjointed as it is unfolding. Everyone is getting part of the story, but few are viewing the whole.

Just as the individual is evolving and bringing all aspects of its split-level spirit-self, to integrate with its multi-layered, multi-conscious soul-self, so too, do all beliefs need to come together, like colours of the rainbow, to embrace the commonality, whilst celebrating the difference. We do not want to merge and dissolve our colours physically to create a muddy sludge, we want to celebrate each colour, let their light shine individually, and together. Celebrating the difference of each colour, whilst noting that when shining together they create the perfect white light, the light that created all, and is contained in all.

We must dissolve the barriers and the structures, and support growth by gently nurturing it instead. To bring beliefs, energy workers/spiritual workers and science together to see the commonality, whilst celebrating the difference, to support and nurture the evolution. Singularly we will struggle, together we will evolve.

The light within every heart is the same – let's begin there.

Let's work from the inside out.

Let's begin from the unity of the light and work outwards towards the differences on the surface of the human experience, rather than beginning with the differences on the surface, and never seeing past this barrier to the oneness that sits at the centre of this.

Working from the inside out works both for humans, and for beliefs.

Let's begin at the Oneness and then radiate out to celebrate the difference.

We are all part of the same light.

Let's begin there,

in togetherness,

all as One.

Whole.

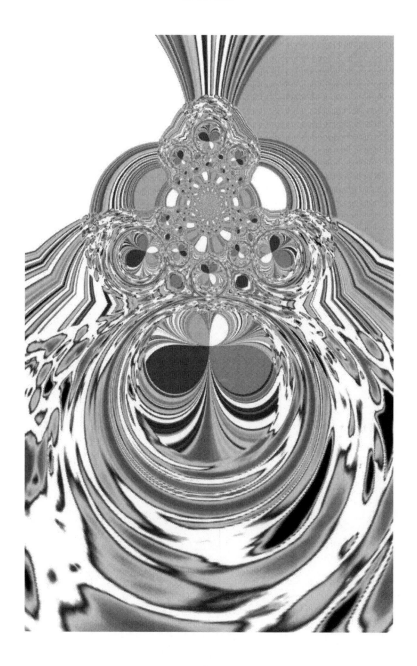

Mel Cross

WHY SHOULD WE EVOLVE?

From 'Passive Receiver'
(Spirit-self) to 'Dynamic
Creator' (Soul-self)

At present, we exist as passive receivers of information. We are physical, emotional and mind in human form, with our spirit-self (incarnate facet of soul) at the centre of this. In our current form (created-self), information is fed into our mind through our programming, our learning, our feelings and our experiences. These things shape us in our created-self. They make us who we believe ourselves to be.

What we learn but do not hold in conscious memory will pass into our unconscious, which is held within soul-self. Our conscious created-self decides what information, learning or experiences etc. are to be held on to, or let go of, as our created-self has finite capacity. But our soul-self has infinite capacity. Our created-self does not know what it is that we truly need, but what we truly need is always understood and known within the soul.

Our soul (Dynamic Creator) is always passing information to our spirit-self (Passive Receiver), to reach our unawake created-self, to guide and inform us. Our soul is always passing us information that we need, in its infinite knowing, to try to help us and to try to make us aware of its presence.

Our created-self holds on to what it believes it needs. Our soul-self holds all and pulls our understanding and experiences together in unique and creative ways. Because soul flows with infinite knowing, is multi-layered, multi-conscious and interconnected, it has the potential for infinite, dynamic, creative output.

In our 'created-self' state we believe we know best and live within the constraints put upon us by current and past thinking, our conditioning, our society and ourselves. As soul there are no barriers and no constructed routes to anything. Everything just *is* and can come together in a myriad of ways. This constantly flowing and evolving state of creation within the soul passes its knowing to our spirit-self within our created-self. It can be felt as creative inspiration, insight, spiritual experience, or knowing beyond knowing.

In the past, many giant leaps of understanding, for example in medicine, theology, science, arts etc. have come from individuals who were able to hear the teaching of their own soul, and flow with their own connection to the infinite grid of all that 'Is', was and will be. Humanity has evolved due to many unique individuals connecting to their own true soul nature.

When a lifetime (or many lifetimes) of facts, information, learning, education and knowledge is mixed with the infinite possibility of our soul, and our dynamic connection to the creative, flowing, that which 'Is', as a Dynamic Creator, we have the potential for all things. With this we can find creative solutions to environmental issues, healthcare, societal problems, political chaos, climate change, energy shortages, humanitarian problems and all manner of things. Individuals can work as a dynamic creator in their own area of expertise, bringing their own unique understanding, developments and breakthroughs, for the evolution and nurturing of all that is in our world. This includes alternatives to our predisposition for war, via discussion and harmonious co-operation. We have everything we need for us to save ourselves from our own selfish, egoic, greedy, heartless, loveless self-destruction. We have plundered and ravaged our planet and people to the brink of destruction. We now have the potential, as Dynamic Creators, to bring it back to a state of equilibrium, of harmony, peace, love and togetherness, both of people, environment and faiths.

It is now our choice.

The route to this state of being has been explained in many ways, in many faiths, but the time has now come to pick up the baton with both hands and walk forward together. The importance of this has never been so imperative to the survival of humanity and the care of our planet and everything in it.

We all wander and wonder what we can do, and how can we possibly make a difference? What's the point? Is it too late?

The point is this.

Whilst we remain Passive Receivers of information from our souls, whilst we remain our created-selves living within the physical, emotions and mind, we are restricted, stifled and separate from the tools, information, love and understanding that we need; both as an individual, and as humankind. When we take that step and begin the journey to incarnate our soul, our Dynamic Creator, we work towards bringing all that we are, all that we know, and all the potential of our unique aspect of the divine, into this body, in this lifetime. We bring everything we deem not possible into the potential of possible. We can all bring our gifts and do our bit for the whole. For everyone and everything. All bringing our unique pieces of the puzzle to help create the picture of the new whole.

We can also share our 'Is'-being, radiating peace, love and light. And through this *being* as true-soul, we can illuminate others, inspire, raise the vibration of all around us, and truly make a difference. If we truly love humankind, if we truly love our world and every beautiful thing within it, if we want true peace and love at every level of our life, and the life of every being, then we can do it – together.

We have a choice.

Do we walk bound and blind-folded in despair, separate and alone, feeling hopeless and helpless as we watch our lives and our world crumble? Or do we take a step and begin to walk towards being the change. The change we want, and the change the world needs. We need to be brave and walk. 'Is' walks with us, 'Is' holds our hand, 'Is' guides our way. Not through conscious projection, but because 'Is' is.

We are never alone.

We are just journeying to find ourselves, and within ourselves is our own unique divine connection to that which 'Is'.

We can do it.

We can exist as love, be love and share love.

It is our choice.

Passive Receiver or Dynamic Creator?

It is not an easy road, but the destination my friends is beyond comprehension, beyond beauty, beyond words and beyond description.

It is pure Love, pure soul, pure 'Is'.

It is you.

My only hope and constant prayer is that it is purity, love and connection to each other that stimulates the change. To feel the need and the benefit, before a trigger or situation forces us into action. That the change comes from love and not fear, from passion to make the world a better place, rather than because of destruction and devastation.

The change will come, either way, but I pray it comes from the medium of peace and love, rather than any other catalyst.

Choose Love.

Truth

There is an explanation for all of this – but not one
easily heard, digested or comprehended, by
the miniscule understanding of the human
mind.
It is the Truth.
The pure and simple Truth.
It is the Truth of all that is,
all that was,
and all that ever will be.

It is the time, the place, the space and the moment, to
sow the seeds of this Truth into the hearts
and souls, and we hope minds, of all
humans.
It is the seed of Truth which will stop lies, and greed,
and violence.
The seed which will stop damage, destruction, and
pollution.
The seed which will stop hatred, conflict, confusion
and pain.

It will bring clarity, understanding and Truth.
It will be simple,
it will be calm
and it will be obvious...
It is, and always has been, obvious.
The blinding light of understanding.

Understanding at the highest level,
Soul level,
'Is' level.

It will not exclude, it will not alienate, it will not
segregate.
It will bring light into souls which spreads the simple
Truth into the hearts of other souls.
The souls whose aching hearts know there is 'more'.
Whose hearts drum to a beat which speaks to them 'I
must do something'...
The beat which speaks of beauty, of peace, of
understanding.
Of connection, community and the joining together of
all humans.
The joining together of humanity, of nature, and of all
things in this most beautiful and precious
World.
The World where the light and love of 'Is' permeates
all things,
lights all things,
and *is* all things.

The disharmony we sense which eats at us and
overwhelms us, it seems right now, to be
irreversible, unstoppable and king.
But it is not.

The time has come to decide,

IS-BEING

do we believe we can change the World,
or do we let it disintegrate?
Do we hold up our hands in despair and defeat?
Or do we hold up our hands and say,
'Yes! I am here, it is time....'

And as each individual hand offers itself, its gifts, its
        light,
it brings hope.
And hope and light shine out.
And then more hands tentatively raise until,
at some point soon,
the hands become a sea,
an ocean,
a tsunami of love, light and change.

They will speak of hope and light and Truth.
All we have is Truth.
And,
My beautiful friends,
There is only one Truth......
......and that Truth is
Love....

SOUL
INTEGRATION

Basic stages of the

process

There is a process to be embarked upon to live as our soul incarnate Dynamic Creator. The basic progression through the stages of this process are discussed in this chapter and will be discussed in more depth later. They are written about in the briefest of ways, to illustrate in the most stripped-back way possible. This is for simplicity, and so that the echoes of this process within faiths and beliefs can be recognised and heard. This process has been worked through in many ways, at many times, within many faiths and no faiths. It is a process unknowingly undertaken when we quest to understand or find ourselves, or when we follow the path of love. When we walk in love, share love and be love, we are already journeying towards our Truth, and the Truth of that which 'Is'.

The process I set out to share with you is from my own knowing and via my own journey through, and beyond, the process. It is from experience, and not learned.

It is what I was guided through in love, faith, trust, truth, surrender, stillness and humility towards the truth of my soul, by the divine light of that which 'Is'. I walked the living process to be able to understand and share, with those who are ready to walk in their own truth, with their own unique connection to their divine spark of that which 'Is'.

Connection to heart-space

This is the first and most important stage. This is when one begins to sense one's connection to *all*, one's connection to healing and love, and where one begins to sense the *Truth* of the process. It is where we begin to sense the gate to our soul, and our connection to our own unique aspect of that which 'Is'.

Living as heart-space resonates at the vibration of healing, interconnectivity and love. If we do nothing else but work at living in, and from, this space, we are already making a difference.

We are already sharing healing with all.

This will affect everything.

Living at heart-space causes us to live as *we* instead of *me*.

Heart-space is where we connect to all.

Heart-space is living as, living with, and living in, Love.

Dissolving the three lower levels of vibration

The three lower levels of our energy field are physical, emotional and mental/mind layers. These are the layers which only exist when we physically incarnate. They are where our personality, experiences and programming are held in this lifetime. When we dissolve the definition of these layers, we create fluidity and a harmonious space in which true-soul can incarnate. We remove false created-self to connect to our soul. This dissolving removes programming and held coagulated, discordant energy due to experiences within this lifetime causing us disharmony or pain.

This process increases our sensitivity to picking up discordancy and enables the stripping back of every disharmony back to birth, to create the right environment for soul to integrate in the re-birthing process.

Connecting the light within heart-space to the light of the soul

The cord of light connection, to that which 'Is' above, runs from 'Is', down through the layers of vibration into soul, where your unique divine aspect of that which 'Is' resides (the 'Is' within). The cord of light runs from the 'Is' within soul, to the incarnate spirit-self within our physical incarnation. The end of this cord resides in the incarnate heart-space. This cord of 'Is' is what links us from that which 'Is' within, to that which 'Is' above. The thread of light within this cord threads down through every energy centre to connect them, and downwards connecting them to the earth. The thread within the cord runs from that which 'Is' above, down to the earth, like an anchor.

When we try to integrate our spirit-self with our soul, we need to recognise their connection. This connection is the light-thread through and within this cord. The light-thread/cord connection is where information is passed from soul, to spirit-self, and vice-versa. When we recognise this link and work with it, we strengthen the connection between spirit-self and soul. It is the link which enables integration to take place. This link, the cord of light, is 'faith'. (Not the faith of any particular religion, but faith in that which 'Is'. Faith – the unseen link.)

Spirit-self integrates with soul, and pulls down, via the cord of light, to incarnate in this lifetime

When layers are fluid, spirit-self can integrate with soul. This eventually happens when there is strong enough communication between your spirit-self and soul, and when you have made the flip between living at the vibration of heart-space, rather than visiting heart-space. Also, when you have resolved nearly all discordant coagulated energy at your physical, emotional and mind layers of vibrational existence, and you have dissolved the barriers between the lower three layers, so that you have free-flowing energetic movement between them.

When there is free-flowing energetic movement and you are existing as heart-space, you have created the environment for soul to exist. This is when your tests will be the hardest; when you are closest to soul integration.

If you can walk through the darkness in total love, total faith, total trust, truth, humility and stillness, and in complete surrender to that which 'Is', your spirit-self will reintegrate with soul. And you will begin to exist as soul-self. The cord of light from spirit-self heart-space to the centre of soul's unique divine aspect of that which 'Is', pulls soul down to incarnate in this lifetime. Your divine light will reside within you, consciously. You will be your fully expansive, fully integrated, multi-vibrational, multi-connected, multi-conscious self. This cannot be achieved with your gaze anywhere other than towards that which 'Is', in love, faith, trust, truth, surrender, stillness and humility.

It has been designed this way.

It keeps soul-self and your unique divine aspect of that which 'Is', safe and separate from the discordant nature of incarnation.

Harmony is the only way to soul, and the process of soul integration is simple, but hard, and ultimately dark, until it is light.

Therefore, the egoic nature of humanity cannot reach its truth or potential until it releases itself from its own grip and walks naked in its faith of that which 'Is', and purely in love.

There is no other way.

◆ ◆ ◆

The journey towards soul integration is totally <u>unique</u> for everyone; there is no 'one way'. Therefore, each individual's journey must be supported, nurtured and not dictated. It is for everyone to find their own path, but the path needs to include the constituent stages in order to arrive at the destination of integration; becoming soul-self, Dynamic Creator.

That said, the process is always swathed in contradictions, and contradiction keeps balance, balance creates harmony.

Each individual embarking on the journey to soul integration will find it unique to them; and rightly so. Each individual is a unique divine aspect of that which 'Is', therefore each journey is different. Everyone's life experiences and programming from circumstance is unique to them. And each person's discordant energy and coagulated energetic experience will be different. Therefore, the journey towards harmonisation and cleansing of self will require different ways and different support. Everyone, once listening to their own *Truth* and their own spiritual experience, will be guided uniquely in a way best for them. Of course, there is the commonality of the stages of the process, and the commonality of the key things which need to be nurtured and embraced in order to get there. But the individual's path will ultimately be unique to them. This is why the instruction may seem general. This is because it is only an armature, to be built upon in an infinite number of ways according to the people taking steps to walk their own unique path.

I sense that a place for people to meet, discuss, *be*, and be guided by experienced, integrated souls, would be the preference for moving forward with this. That is until the individual is working in clarity with their own soul-self, and that which 'Is', who will guide them through their own process. It is our aim to help nurture them until they are up and running on their own, with inner *Truth*, and a clear, sensitive, energy system.

We will be the stabilisers on the bicycle, until they can be taken off and you can ride freely and alone. How you ride a bicycle cannot be articulated, only felt – much like this journey!

Therefore, this book is written with simplicity of description and process for you to fill in the experiences, the knowledge, the beliefs, and the knowing for yourself. It is only the bones of things.

This is because the old is changing. This is because if we try to encase this knowing within the old structures, we bring its vibration down to the mind and lose its freedom and potential. Work it alongside, and with, what you already understand; explore and grow. But keep it simple, because simple is the only way. Simple is in the heart not in the head. Learn and unlearn. Hold then let go. Knowing is in your heart, knowing will not be found in your head.

Whilst I was being made consciously aware of this information, I began to research the energy system (for about 10 minutes!) but very firmly felt NO! Do not find previous 'facts' to substantiate what is being understood.

It must be pure.

If you wish to research and flesh out this understanding, please do. But remember to trust your knowing. If it doesn't feel right, it is because it is not right. If your teacher is from ego you will feel it. If they are from love, you will feel it. Trust, and you will be guided. It is all about love, faith, trust, truth, surrender, stillness and humility. This is all you need to find your way. But I am sure you will find those you need when you need them, to help you on your path and keep you focussed on the light of that which 'Is'. This is where the fundamentals of the journey are learned.

The journey is for you, and walked by you. We can guide, advise, and help, but ultimately, we walk alone, hand in hand with that which 'Is'. Just walk and the path will appear at your feet.

The Mirage

When we are aware that we are a spiritual being, we
wander the spiritual desert searching for
sustenance.
There are two things we may find: An oasis, or a
mirage.

If we happen across an oasis, we will feel revitalised,
refreshed, renewed.
We will benefit from the sparkling waters of wisdom,
of clarity, of enlightenment.
We will continue our journey anew, shining brightly as
we go on our way, having learned and having
grown.

If we come across a mirage,
no matter how big it is,
how much it shimmers,
or no matter how loudly it shouts,
it is not an oasis... it is a mirage.
If you drink at an oasis, and every time you do, you fill
your mouth with the driest of sand; this is a
mirage.

Learn to distinguish between an oasis and a mirage.
A mirage does not feed you, it feeds from you, and will
eventually take away all that made you shine.

Growth only comes from resting and refreshing at an oasis.

Mel Cross

UNDERSTANDING ASPECTS OF ENERGY

The universal language

U nderstanding aspects of energy - will be explained in a simple way, for ease of understanding for those unfamiliar with energy work, therefore giving a rudimentary introduction to these concepts. Although this is for accessibility, it is also because each person will sense things differently, understand things differently, and interpret things differently. It is for your soul and your divine aspect of 'Is' to guide and help you understand things according to your unique path. That which is written here is explained in a basic way, for you to grow, explore and nurture your own personal understanding.

These energetic concepts are understood and written about in a plethora of ways elsewhere and can be explored further independently.

Layers of vibration

Layers of vibration are talked about throughout this book. There are layers of vibrational frequency from that which 'Is', the highest, purest vibration of love and light, down through all frequencies to that of physical. Each layer as it descends becomes a denser and denser frequency. The word descends is not a judgement of 'place', it is only for visualisation purposes. There are vast numbers of layers each resonating with different aspects of spiritual existence.

The highest level of vibration is that which 'Is' above, then spiritual connection, spiritual communication, heart-space, mind, emotion and physical. There are many other layers beyond, within and between these, and many variations on the interpretations and understanding of these layers. Each layer of vibration has different qualities and connections to different energetic ways of working or being.

For ease of visualisation:
'Is' layer – white (or violet)
Spiritual Connection layer – indigo
Spiritual Communication layer – blue
Heart-space layer – green (or pink)
Mind layer – yellow
Emotion layer – orange
Physical layer – red

These layers correspond to the system of energy centres overlaying and within our physical body and correspond to the layers of our energy field in this physical/created-self/spirit-self incarnation.

Like white light splits to create a rainbow, white 'Is' split to create a rainbow of vibration. Each layer of vibration containing multiple layers and nuances, each connecting spiritually in different ways. Whatever you personally sense with the structure of these layers is your interpretation. It is for you to learn about, and decipher, in a way which suits your beliefs and understanding. This basic description of layers is a start-point to help us sense, connect with, and visualise this energetically layered existence. Understanding the separation and differences between the layers are crucial for energetic working, and for the evolution of your spirit/created-self to soul-self.

We need to understand how our energetic system fits and works within this, both as a separated-layered spirit-being, and as a multi-frequency, combined-layered soul-being.

So, for ease of simplicity in visualisation we shall discuss the layers of vibration in our energy system as follows:

'Is' layer – Highest vibration, purity, love and light.

Spiritual Connection layer – Where we can access spiritual existence/aspects of that which exists in a non-tangible physical world.

Spiritual Communication layer – Vibration of communication. Where our *truth* and divine *truth* communicate to us.

Heart-space layer – Connection to vibration of love, interconnection, connection to healing, connection to 'Is' within, connection to soul. Where divine truth, and our truth, is sensed.

Mind layer – Vibration of mind/thought.

Emotion layer – Vibration of emotion/human feeling.

Physical layer – Vibration of physical requirement in a physical world. Vibration of ancestral memory.

As a physical/created-self/spirit-self the physical layer is closest to our physical body, with the other layers radiating out from this; 'Is' layer being the furthest away from our physical body. When we become dynamic creator soul-self incarnate these layers reverse in our energy field, with 'Is' layer closest to our physical body and other layers radiating out from this; physical layer being furthest from our physical body.

Cord from heart-space to that which 'Is' above

Our energetic system is connected to the 'Is' above (the highest frequency of vibration). The cord of light which connects us is what brings life to us in a physical/spirit-self incarnation and sits within us as a soul. This cord of light from 'Is' comes down through the layers of vibration, connects to soul and our unique aspect of the divine which sits within our soul, and then continues down into the centre of our spirit-self in this incarnation and down into the physical.

This cord of light is what connects us to 'Is' above, our unique aspect of the divine, and connects soul-self and spirit-self.

It is the cord which our conscious gaze travels up and down, to connect to our spiritual nature, soul and 'Is'. Whilst incarnated in the physical body, our conscious gaze is usually directed into the physical, emotional, and mind aspects of that which we are.

The cord is strongest from 'Is' to soul, lesser from soul to spirit-self, and least from spirit-self to physical. Therefore, the further up the cord our conscious gaze is fixed, the more divine connection is felt and understood. This is due to the increased flow of information because of the increased capacity of the connection.

This cord of light needs to be focused upon, and aligned with, for our spiritual path to be walked and our divine connection nurtured, grown and expressed. This can be done by working with the supporting 'Principles of Connection' discussed in a later chapter. When our focus wanders from our divine light cord connection, we lose sight of that which we are, and that which we strive to evolve towards, and we become lost within our 'created-self' and our created world.

Energy Centres (access points)

There is much talk about energy centres, what they are, where they are and what they do.

Energy centres are located within our energetic system. Each of these centres are links/access points to our own energy system, our energy field, and to external levels of vibration. These energy centres are in a straight line, from the base of our body, to the crown of our head. (They are also located below this and above this and can also be found all over the energetic system.)

In many traditional systems of energy work, the energy centres are explained as follows (From lowest located between the legs (base), to the highest located at the crown of the head):

Crown centre: White (or violet). Relates to our connection to the divine
Brow centre: Indigo. Relates to spirituality
Throat centre: Blue. Relates to communication
Heart centre: Green (or pink). Relates to love/healing
Solar plexus centre: Yellow. Relates to mind/me
Sacral centre: Orange. Relates to emotions
Base centre: Red. Relates to physical

The energy centres are connected to, and aligned with, the layers of vibration of our energy system around our physical form. When incarnated in a physical form the physical layer (corresponding to the base centre) is closest to the physical body, then the emotional layer (corresponding to the sacral centre), then the mind layer (corresponding to the solar plexus centre) etc, with all the layers up to 'Is' layer (corresponding to crown centre).

These energy centres connect to the layers of our energy field, and all layers of vibration up through the cord of connection to that which 'Is'. These energy centres are like access points. If our conscious intent focuses on our emotional centre, for example, we connect to all aspects and experiences of our incarnated-self held within the emotional level of our energy field. We can also connect through the emotional centre to the emotional layer of vibration between that which 'Is' and the physical. They all correspond with each other.

There are, in fact, many energy centres located in our system, which connect to many aspects of us as an energetic being, and the corresponding layers of vibration. There is an energy centre which corresponds to each layer of vibration, all the way up our energetic cord, for us to have the potential to consciously connect to all things. But, until we evolve to be able to comprehend what is potentially accessible further up the layers of vibration, we will not be able to consciously access them unless 'Is' allows this access. And there is a reason for this. If we could access this high-level spiritual connection, from a standing start of physical, emotional and mind existence, as we currently are, it would be too much for us to be able to cope with and could create mental imbalance. We are also not able to access this information/connection in our current make-up, because our senses and our brains are not currently set up to receive and translate such information. Therefore, we need to evolve into multi-vibrational, multi-conscious, multi-connected souls, so that access to, and translation of, higher-level understanding can take place. And even then, as an incarnate soul, it will still be inhibited by our physical form and our capacity to interpret and comprehend the spiritual information received. Physical existence creates restrictions.

There is much discussion by energy workers, at present, about the evolution of the energy system and new energy centres being connected to and understood. This is all wonderful, but this is an evolving system with an evolving destination. The discovery of new energy centres comes with our upgraded capacity to sense and interpret higher evolved information. This is due to the raising of the vibration of the planet, and the sensitivity of individuals moving up the bandwidth to experience higher connections and understandings, and therefore receiving more evolved information.

This is the transitioning process as we evolve from heart-space living, to dissolve lower-level frequencies, which enables fluidity for connection to soul-self, which brings conscious connection of spirit-self heart-space to soul-self divine aspect, via the cord of light. This process concludes with the full integration of spirit-self and soul, with soul finally incarnating. As this process takes place, greater connection to higher levels of vibration will be experienced, via the evolving higher-level energy centres being sensed and accessed. But this is transitional.

Once full soul/spirit-self integration has taken place, and soul has incarnated, our energetic system will exist as one major energy centre working at all levels of frequency. This is because we will be functioning as multi-vibrational, multi-functioning, multi-conscious soul. Therefore, one energy centre contains all centres, one soul contains multiple layers of frequencies existing at the same time in harmony (rather than separated layers). The one centre can be separated into its constituent parts for specific work, or to focus on one level of vibration, but then will merge back into one. The separate centres are no longer required as we are no longer separate layers of vibration, we are multi-vibrational.

But, as I said, we will not be able to fully access the highest levels of vibration due to our physical existence, restricted receiving equipment, and our limited ability to interpret that which 'Is' whilst physically incarnate.

We may not be able to interpret that which 'Is' (as interpretation happens within the mind), but that which 'Is' is sensed within the soul as love, light, peace and joy; this is all we need.

As our bodies and brains evolve to accommodate this new energetic existence, our capacity to receive, understand, and comprehend will increase, and the evolutionary process of humankind will flourish. This increase in capacity is because instead of receiving information, we will be existing *within* information. Our *being* will be in constant flow of potential and potential information.

This may seem very complex to those who have not experienced energy work, or who have not come across any of the beliefs or traditions which incorporate this understanding. But bear with it! I shall endeavour to bring some clarity to this.

The need for an understanding of energy work

It is essential as we evolve towards peace, love, and harmony, that our understanding of energy work increases; but increases in a safe and nurturing way. It seems, in many societies, it has been separated from mainstream understanding and brushed under the carpet, only to be explored by 'seekers' of understanding. But this separation and disconnection has pushed us further and further away from our connection to our true-soul, and our connection to that which 'Is'. If we move forward and evolve, we need to understand, establish connections to, and learn to work with 'energy'. This causes the bringing of many gifts and understanding, but if incorrectly learned, or worked with, can lead to misuse and misfortune.

If used for the benefit of all of creation, energy work should be the conscious co-operation with that which 'Is', by us, to bring harmony, healing, peace and love. Not through the guidance of our mind, but from the guidance of our heart. This is achieved by conscious connection to our soul, and by consciously receiving information from the flowing, dynamic spirit of that which 'Is', and from that which 'Is' above.

This has all been done throughout history in many ways, using different methods and vocabulary, from peoples of all beliefs and none. Some belief systems have shunned this, hidden it, or separated it. Some have embraced it and worked at understanding, working with, and interpreting it. It is now time to share a greater understanding of energy work, so that humankind can harness and work with our magnificent potential, and so that we can play our unique parts in facilitating the evolution of mankind. But this understanding needs to be clear, to be nurtured, and to be shared by those who understand what is necessary to evolve from spirit into soul.

There are many energy workers who 'think' they know best. But things are changing, and we are changing. Old methods and ways of working are changing. Those who are truly *listening* will walk in the right direction. Those who *hear* but do not *listen*, and who *think* they know, will walk in circles. Those who *think* they know are working from ego and are not stepping towards evolution. Those who dictate are lost. Those who help you by nurturing *your* own 'truth' and *your* own connection to guidance, are the ones to walk beside. Those who support and nurture, are the greatest gardeners of all; their motives are to help you to grow and flower, rather than take from you and grow their own importance.

We need to create a space/place for ordinary folk to connect to and understand that which they are, that which they could be, and that we are all connected – all One. This is done through understanding the fundamentals of energy work and nurturing and expanding ones knowing of that which 'Is'.

There are many incredible people out there who can guide you on your path; choose wisely.

Understanding energy will help all that is written about in this book to make more sense and will help you evolve into your own true soul.

Bringing together belief systems, energy workers and science, to work together towards a greater understanding of this evolutionary process, will bring about the evolution of mankind.

Separate we will fail, together we will evolve.

Energy work for clearing, cleansing, harmonising and increasing sensitivity

Energy work needs to be understood for us to begin clearing ourselves and our environment. When we are sensitive to our energy system, we notice changes within it, and how it affects us mentally, emotionally and physically. By being sensitive to our energy we can begin to sense when we are out of balance, when something is affecting us, and when we are discordant. Through this understanding and sensitivity, we can begin to address these issues, situations, and experiences to harmonise them, and ultimately to harmonise ourselves. If we are not able to sense that which affects us, we will not know what it is that we need to work on to clear disharmonious energy.

Through energy work we can clear the discordant energy we accumulate as we go about our lives. Sometimes we pick up negativity from people, places or situations. This negative energy, if left unaddressed, may go of its own accord, or may not. If it does not go it can affect us, leaving us clogged, heavy or exhausted. If left for too long, it can begin to affect us further. If we are aware of how to sense our energy system and how to clear/cleanse it, we create a space of clarity, harmony and balance from which to work, and with which to sense more accurately.

Walking through life with an energy system which is not cleared, is like trying to view life through a very dirty window.

When we begin to work with energy, we can learn to protect ourselves and our energy system from discordant energy. We can keep our energy system clear and 'unpolluted'. We can also learn methods to negate negativity and negative influence, from those people/situations/places and spiritual influence which cause disharmony and hinder our evolution.

Learning to work with our energetic system will allow us to be able to sense the different layers of vibration and enables us to consciously connect to these layers of vibration. This will facilitate us connecting to spiritual information and guidance. It will enable us to begin to sense our heart-space, the gate to our soul, our interconnected nature, and our connection to our unique aspect of the divine.

When we begin to understand energy work our sensitivity increases, and this enables us to more consciously work at walking our path to soul integration. We will be able to sense our 'truth' and what is discordant. We will be able to identify what affects us, and work towards removing that which restricts, distracts and causes disharmony.

Through energy work we will be able to identify, dissolve and harmonise coagulated energy within our system. We will notice when something 'flags up' as needing to be addressed. We will be able to identify what it is, where it is, and how we can deal with it. The removal of discordant coagulations enables our vibration to raise, increases fluidity of energy movement within our energy field, and brings a greater increase in sensitivity. This brings about even greater fine-tuning of our energetic system. The more sensitive you are, the more you identify and deal with; the more you identify and deal with, the more sensitive you become, and on it goes.

When you work with energy you can identify energetic ties and cords which are holding you in place, and holding you from growth, raised vibration and evolution. These energetic ties can be to people, situations, past experiences, and aspects of created-self. When we are energetically sensitive, we can remove unwanted cords and attachments and follow cords to see where they originate from. When we can follow a thread back and back to the original source of current behaviour, thinking and circumstance, we can address, heal and harmonise it.

Within life, energy work naturally takes place. Working with love, faith, trust, truth, surrender, stillness and humility we will heal and cleanse energetically, without consciously realising or understanding. These ideals are often an integral part of belief systems, and they are the ideals which help us on our path to that which 'Is'. With dedication to walking this path, cleansing, healing and protection take place. And, even though we may not realise it, we work through and resolve many energetic issues in prayer or meditation, through conscious focus, and by sitting in the vibration of love. Even with no belief system, by us living as genuinely kind, compassionate and loving people, we can create harmony within our system through conscious intent and direction.

Conscious direction of thought creates energetic change.

Energetic change is facilitated by that which 'Is', the dynamic, creative aspect of 'Is' and our 'Is' within. Also, our soul is always trying to heal, help, and guide us, which also brings about energetic change.

If, with humility and greatest gratitude, we work *with* that which 'Is' to consciously take responsibility for our own energetic system, to treat it with care and respect, and consciously create the best possible energetic 'temple' to house our unique divine aspect, this is the greatest gift we can give to that which 'Is', to our soul-self and to humanity.

If we consciously work to help nurture our energetic system, by listening to our 'truth' and soul/Is direction, we are working towards our own evolution, and this, in turn, will encourage the evolution of others. What we do to the one, affects the *All*.

If we work to nurture our energetic system from 'mind' we will trip up. Remember, *mind* does not know what is best. Listen to the *truth* within your own soul and create your own unique temple. Some may say it is up to that which 'Is' to do what is necessary – but the time has come for us to consciously connect to that which 'Is', in order to assist and help facilitate our own growth. Not for our own false glory, but to share the ultimate glory of that which 'Is'. We have too long been the 'Passive Receiver'. We must now evolve towards being a 'Dynamic Creator', and take responsibility for becoming, and being, the change we want to see. We must try to work as a conscious facilitator, to enable that which 'Is' to illuminate and shine brightly with love and light via our own unique aspect of the divine.

Don't wait for the change to come to you.
Walk towards the change.
Be the change...

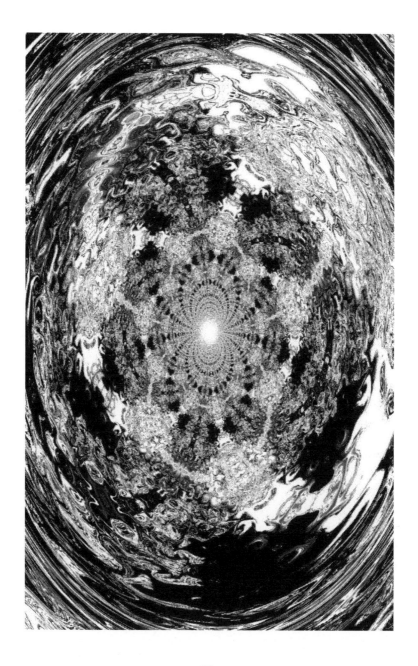

Mel Cross

PASSIVE RECEIVER

Spirit-self incarnate

I n this chapter I will discuss how the physical human being exists as a spirit-self incarnate Passive Receiver and why it is necessary to begin the evolution towards heart-space existence and eventually soul-integration; existing as soul-self incarnate, Dynamic Creator.

Spirit-self incarnate:
The three lower levels of Passive Receiver

When we exist as soul we exist as multi-vibrational, multi-layered, multi-conscious, multi-connected energy. When this multi-existing soul separates a facet of itself to create spirit-self to incarnate into a physical existence, the layers of vibration separate. A physical, emotional and mind layer are pulled in and created by soul, for the facet of soul (spirit-self) to incarnate.

The physical, emotional, then mind layers of vibration, when incarnate, are closest to the physical body. They are the layers which create our personality in this lifetime. They hold unresolved coagulated energy from previous lifetimes which we need to work through in this lifetime. As the physical, emotional, and mind layers do not exist within the multi-vibrational soul, the discordant energy from previous incarnations are held on the outer layer of soul. This is what causes disharmony to the soul.

So, as an incarnate spirit-self, our conscious gaze must find its way through the physical, emotional, and mind layers of existence, to be able to consciously touch the heart-space layer of vibration, as these are the layers that are closest to us as a physical being. The heart-space layer is the one in which we begin to be aware that we are not just a physical, emotional, mind-based human being. It is within these three lower layers that we are influenced and manipulated by everything around us, and everything that we have experienced in this lifetime. It is where programming takes place and is held. It is where our created-self is held. These layers block us from seeing the truth of our soul and the light of that which 'Is'. These layers are like three walls which we try to see over, break through, and dismantle, to try and glimpse 'truth'.

When our conscious gaze exists in the ever-restrictive straight-jacket of the physical, emotional and mind layers, we are only able to be a Passive Receiver of information from our soul-self and from that which 'Is'. Or we direct our conscious gaze, when we are more aware, to seek information and try to connect to our *knowing*. We do not sit within knowing, as a soul-self incarnate does. Our connection to our soul-self and 'Is', is difficult to glimpse, and even harder to maintain, when we are a Passive Receiver.

Physical level vibration:
The first level of incarnate existence

The first layer of existence is our physical level vibration, which is the layer closest to our physical body. It is the layer of physicality and physical requirement. It is the layer where fundamental requirements for existence are acknowledged. It is where disharmony of physical experience is held. It is where we connect to the physical existence of matter and where we understand its fundamental effect on us as a human and energetic being. It is where ancestral memory and energetic-genetic programming is held (energetic patterns passed down through ancestors). It is also where physical experience, and physical experience from previous incarnations, can be held to be resolved and harmonised. All traumatic physical experience which is not dropped at the point of passing over can be held in the external layer of the soul to be harmonised.

With the new shift in bandwidth of energetic frequencies, the continued cycle of coagulation re-emergence and resolution will no longer be required if we have incarnated soul-self in this lifetime. When we exist at heart-space frequency we are at the vibration of constant healing. This is how low-level physical past-life coagulated energies and old patterns will begin to be dissolved. Whilst living in heart-space frequency as soul, low-level coagulated disharmonious energy at a physical level will be dissolved through constant clearing. It is also easier to identify because of high-level sensitivity and conscious connection to vibrational disturbance. Therefore, all physical disharmony in soul incarnate state will have instant clearance and not pass through into further lives of soul progression. This will accelerate the progression of one's soul evolution.

This constant harmonisation, when incarnated as soul-self, is also true of the emotional and mind layers.

The physical layer of vibration is where we connect to spirits which have passed over and reintegrated back into soul. For a soul to communicate to us in a physical existence it must manifest at a level closest to us – at the energetic physical level. A soul must create an energetic image/pattern of the human it is representing for us to recognise it. This is how those who have passed are able to show themselves visually as they were, at any point in that lifetime. Soul can recreate the 'human' of a certain lifetime as it has uploaded information and memory experiences of that lifetime into the true soul-self.

When you are existing as spirit-self within your created-self, at the point of passing over, all relevant information and experiences which have not already been passed to soul, will be uploaded into soul. When you are existing as a soul within this lifetime, this uploading is no longer required at the time of passing over, as this information is directly within soul.

When we pass over, we drop the three lower levels of frequency – physical, emotional, and mind. The information from these levels is uploaded into soul-self. If the three lower levels are not dissolved successfully after the uploading and are caught in the energetic fabric of 'place', this is what we experience as ghosts. The energetic representation of the human in that lifetime captured until it naturally dissolves, or is harmonised by that which 'Is' or an energy worker. This is different to a spirit.

A spirit witnessed on the earth plane (other than those who re-represent back from soul to communicate or guide) is the incarnate aspect of a soul's spirit-self, still trapped within its human identity, and not re-integrated into pure soul-self. The stuck spirit is the fragment of soul which incarnated in that lifetime. The spirit is usually stuck due to traumatic passing, unresolved earthbound issues, energetic tethering by those still alive, or fearful of judgement/going to the light. The spirit does not recognise it is part of, but separate from, its soul-self, doesn't want to reintegrate, or cannot reintegrate. This is because some aspects of emotional or mental frequencies have not been fully separated or dissolved and still connect to lower-level frequencies and physical existence. The stuck spirit can reintegrate once issues are resolved, fear removed, energetic ties dissolved, or stuck lower levels harmonised. Fear to go towards the light can sometimes be indicative of tethering, or lack of dissolving of lower frequencies, as fear is an emotional/mental frequency.

The light experienced at the point of passing is the re-integration of spirit-self into soul, and soul's direct connection to that which 'Is'. The tunnel of light experienced is the single layered consciousness travelling up the light cord into true-soul. The peace experienced is the multi-vibrational harmonious soul-self, and the recognition of the connection to that which 'Is'.

If we have already integrated our spirit-self into soul by dissolving our created-self, stuck spirit-self will no longer be an issue.

Emotional level vibration:
The second level of incarnate existence

This is the emotional level of existence, where we live as an emotional being. This is where we feel things that stimulate us into action, whether this be positive or negative feelings, or positive or negative actions. As humans, our emotions are what drive us to do things and act. They are the signposts of things which need to be addressed.

When we have physical damage, it creates pain to protect ourselves and gives instruction that we need to act. For instance, if we burn our hand on the oven it produces 2 types of pain. The first pain makes us take instant action to save our hand. The second pain is the long, lingering, constant pain from the wound. This is to remind us not to do the same thing again. It reminds us to be cautious and protects us from repeating the action. These pains are signposts and reminders.

Our emotions are also signposts and reminders. They direct us to act if we are emotionally distressed, and they tell us when things are positive, to remind us what actions are positive and beneficial to our emotional well-being. When we do not act to remedy the negative emotional signposts, we become distressed and eventually this can lead to depression or another stronger reminder or signpost of emotional disharmony. These experiences of emotional disharmony can cause disharmonious coagulations of energy in the energetic system. Therefore, it is important, if possible, to work on signposts physically, practically, emotionally, mentally and energetically. Because they all work together to harmonise the issues underlying the signposts of disharmony.

The level of emotional vibration is where we store disharmonious coagulations of energy from emotional trauma, which we have not dealt with. If we harmonise these emotions in a practical, emotional or mental way this can dissolve the energetic coagulations. But sometimes energetic healing needs to take place too for the issue to be fully cleared. Healing alone can remove energetic coagulations caused by emotional trauma, but without working at a practical, emotional and mental level, the causes, triggers, behaviours and reactions which caused the trauma in the first place, have not been removed. Therefore, the coagulation may well return. It is up to us to take responsibility for our wellbeing and we need to consciously be ready to work on dissolving disharmony and letting things go.

Emotional trauma which is disharmonious to the soul may be held in the energetic system until it is harmonised. Emotions help us identify what needs to be addressed. These are signposts. Anything that creates emotion, or reaction, is to help us identify something within ourselves which needs attention and harmonisation.

Mind level vibration:
The third level of incarnate existence

The third level of existence is that of the mind. This is where we accumulate facts and knowledge. This is where our ego resides and where our created-self is maintained. This is the level where we believe we 'know' things. This 'knowing' is false. This knowing is created by that which you have learned or understood through everyday life. This 'knowing' is completely different to true *knowing* and is of a completely different vibration. True *knowing* can only be experienced by existing within the heart-space level of vibration, or conscious connection at the heart-space level of vibration. The 'mind' is programable, it is not who we are. It is like a computer which stores, sorts and organises information and experiences.

Spirit-self is the interpreter of information it receives from its soul-self, spirit and 'Is', which it translates for the mind. Mind is not able to receive and process information from these sources without the translation from spirit-self.

Our created-self believes we are our intellect, personality and experiences, which we are as a created human-being. But, when we can sense our spirit-self, begin to exist at the vibration of heart-space, and begin to consciously connect to our soul-self and that which 'Is', we begin to glimpse the eternal, expansive peace and love of our 'truth', and the truth of that which 'Is'.

When we only identify with mind-level and below, our thoughts are a constant source of distraction, and this distraction will keep you in low-level vibration. Your thoughts and your mind will distract and scatter your focus energetically. Whilst the mind is hooked onto thought, soul-self and 'Is' cannot be heard clearly, if at all. The mind is a constant source of disconnection between our created-self and our soul.

The mind should be a reference library, dipped into occasionally to aid soul. Our true natures are not the accumulated knowledge and experience of the 'mind', we are the occasional visitor to the library of information. We are not the books - we visit the books. In fact, we do not even want to 'own' or 'loan' the books, as this ties us to them, cords are constructed, and again we are tethered at the level of mind. We need the framework of the library to grow, but eventually we need to remove the framework to truly reach the light. Observe, respect, let go of, and dissolve the library. This way we are closer to soul-self, true-self and truth itself.

Even thoughts on spiritual experience and that which 'Is' should be let go of. Because thoughts are from the mind, and that which we are trying to connect to is not of the mind, therefore even thoughts on that which 'Is', are the very things which stop us truly connecting to, and experiencing, that which 'Is'.

It is a paradox, we need to let go of that which we desire, to connect to that which we desire.

If any book is required to focus the mind, don't let it be a book let it be a word only. And even then, words have a frequency and resonance themselves. Every word we think creates ripples of energy, which can affect us at many levels. Word and sound bring the no-thing into the beginnings of form. It is the first stage of calcification, of holding vibration into form. If we can go behind and beyond the word, into the formless, infinite void of potential, it is there that which 'Is' is glimpsed, and felt, in its fluid, flowing, knowledge-filled/empty-formless self. Behind and beyond is where the mystery of 'Is' exists. Not as a word, or a sound, but within and beyond it. To grasp the word causes the purity and vibration of that which wishes to be expressed to be dulled and solidified.

To be beyond word, thought, and form, brings us closer to the no-thing, the grid of infinite potential. The free-flowing, life-breath of that which 'Is', through, around and in all things.

The more you strip away, the more you have. The less you 'know', the more you *know*. The emptier you are, the more you contain. The mind and the level of mind vibration is what separates us from our truth, our soul and our conscious connection to that which 'Is'.

♦ ♦ ♦

'Passive Receiver' – Spirit-self incarnate

A Passive Receiver is someone who lives within the limits of lower-level vibrations, as well as working towards accessing higher-level vibrations and information. They are working through dissolving low-level coagulations of energy and working towards existing within heart-space vibration. They are created-self living with their incarnate single-vibrational layered spirit-self. They are only able to consciously connect to one layer of vibration at a time, although this is fluid.

In short, 'Passive Receiver – Spirit-self incarnates' are human beings just 'doing their thing'!

Passive Receivers can be at various stages of the process of soul evolution towards becoming Dynamic Creators – Multi-vibrational, multi-conscious, soul-self incarnate. Each person is special, each path different, each person's way of evolving unique, although the key points within the process are: Connecting to heart-space, living as heart-space, dissolving coagulated energy at the lower three levels of the energetic system, consciously connecting light within heart-space to light within soul, integrating spirit-self back into soul and bringing soul into this lifetime.

To begin with, as a Passive Receiver of information, we are not aware of our connection to our own 'truth' – our soul, our unique aspect of the divine, or our connection to that which 'Is'. We are not consciously aware of the information we receive from soul, or that which 'Is', via our spirit-self. We may receive illuminated thought, creative insight or unexplainable feelings of love, but we do not understand where they originate from. They are fleeting experiences, are not sustained, and are difficult to repeat. Often, we try to repeat the behaviours or circumstances which we believe were conducive to this experience or connection. These become our rituals, or methods of trying to replicate these special experiences. But because we have no understanding of exactly what it was that happened, and we do not understand the energetic mechanics of what happened, we try to repeat the physical, emotional or mental circumstance in which we 'connected'. But, the vibration/space in which we truly made connection cannot be repeated by mind or circumstance alone. It may be experienced again, but it is intermittent, because the true vibration, which brought about this love or connection to one's spirit-self/soul/'Is', came about through entering the vibration of heart-space. When we are Passive Receivers we are cluttered with the physical, emotional, and mind. This creates barriers and blocks to constant fluid connection with that which 'Is', our soul, and the vibrational level of heart-space, which is where we truly connect to these.   Of course, creating ritual, space, or circumstances you *believe* will connect you to that which you previously experienced, may lift you into heart-space vibration. This is because your conscious gaze is upon repeating the experience, but the connection to this vibration is intermittent. When we try to force the experience, this comes from 'mind', and mind vibration is below heart-space vibration; therefore, true constant connection will not be created. When we let go of the place we are trying to reach, and we surrender to the experience, we elevate into the vibration of heart-space. When we *think* connection and insight, we fall short of it into mind vibration.

When we let go, trust and surrender, we are lifted into heart-space, which is where connection is made.

As everyone knows, love cannot be dictated or forced – otherwise it is not true love. If we let it be, let it free, it grows into love, and we grow in to love/heart-space vibration.

When we are Passive Receivers, we use our senses to receive and decipher information. We believe everything we receive via our senses to be the only things which allow us to experience our reality. But our senses and our decoder of senses, our brain, are relatively primitive. When the brain finally begins to evolve and access the areas of itself which are not now used, to create new ways of receiving and processing information, human and spiritual evolution at every level will flourish.

The information we truly need to help our spiritual natures evolve, at present, does not come via our traditional senses. Of course, we have the sensations of hearing, seeing and feeling etc. as sensations of spiritual experience – but instead of the information coming into the brain via these senses, our spirit-self feeds us spiritual experience, and uses these senses to help our brain make sense of the information we have received. It is like our soul, if you only spoke English, speaks a foreign language, then our spirit-self translates and feeds our ears the information in English, otherwise we would make little sense of what we were receiving. We may pick up a word or two, but the rest would be incomprehensible. Some individuals' spirit-selves, as their spiritual journey progresses, become very fluent translators of foreign languages to English, as their tools and constant use of the language eases translation. When we become soul-self incarnate we live multi-lingually, not needing to translate anything. We live as English, and many other nationalities besides.

When we take in information from our perceived reality, as a Passive Receiver, the words enter our ears as English and go straight to our brain. The spirit-self observes and passes the information to soul-self. Soul-self does not need a translation!

Therefore, as a Passive Receiver of information we interpret both internal and external information through receiving them via the senses, or having information translated in a way the senses understand; i.e. Visually, aurally etc.

When we begin to consciously receive information from soul, this information is felt or sensed somewhere other than these senses, and our spirit-self deciphers the information and delivers it to the brain as images that we must then interpret. But essentially information from that which 'Is', our soul-self, and from spirit, are 'felt'. Therefore, it is imperative to keep our energetic systems clear, so that we *feel* or *sense* as clearly as possible, and so that we can distinguish spirit-self information, from information being practically gathered by our five senses.

When we are Passive Receivers we should intentionally *listen* for information and wait to receive it. This information is given to us from the dynamic, creative that which 'Is', soul-self information, or information from spirit (that which is not tangible in a physical world). Our spirit-self translates this into something we can understand, i.e. split-level vibration rather than multi-vibrational. This split-level vibrational information is then translated into a form recognised by our brain and our 'me' or created-self. As our spirit-self and created-self operate as split-level vibration, the information must be translated into split-level vibrational information for translation and understanding as a physical human.

When we begin to recognise the information we receive as coming from somewhere other than our created-self and our senses, we begin to sense our spirit-self and our body as separate but together. This is when we begin exploring our spiritual nature. This is when we may find teachers who are able to help us connect to the information which is passed to us from these levels. But, even though we travel up and down our 'Is' cord of light connection, and access information via the energy centres at these levels, we are still *given* information when we look for it. This is because information is always translated in the spirit-self, to pass into conscious awareness. When we exist as soul-self incarnate, all information is within us as we are multi-vibrational and multi-conscious. We have one energy centre that contains all, and all information is within us. Our soul-self is in constant flow of all vibrations and is consciously connected at all levels. When we are functioning as incarnate true soul-self, the 'Is' grid flows freely within us, and our 'Is' above connection is strong. We are no longer Passive Receivers; we are Dynamic Creators. Just by *being*, we contain all and can share all.

We are not *seekers*; we are *sharers* of that which we have.
We are flowing with *knowing*.

When we are Passive Receivers, we receive information from our spirit guides (we will look at this in more detail later). We work closely with them to develop trust, knowing, and understanding, and they help us develop our sensing and feeling of things. When we receive information, we tend to check with our guides to see if the things we sense, feel, or understand, are correct. When we learn that the information we receive is correct, we begin to develop our trust in our internal sensing/feeling, our receivers of information from our soul-self via our spirit-self. Instead of looking *outside* for confirmation of what we sense, we begin trust our internal sensing. This developing sensitivity is what helps us learn to trust, have faith, and surrender to that which 'Is'. When we recognise this, we know that what we sense, and feel, is helping guide us on our spiritual path, and we then work hard to develop this sensing. This is when we learn to truly trust and truly begin to sense Truth.

Guides and spiritual experiences are signposts towards our spiritual path. They help us on our journey. They confirm our *knowing* and our *sensing*. When we follow our knowing and sensing in love, faith, trust, truth, surrender, stillness and true humility we begin to sense what we need, what we should do, what we need to address within our energy system, and when we are truly in our heart-space.

True *knowing* is first experienced within the vibration of heart-space.

As a Passive Receiver we make conscious connections to layers of vibration in order to receive information. Our spirit-self helps us focus on one layer of vibration at a time. Although our consciousness flows freely and fluidly between layers, our spirit-self helps it focus on one layer to maintain connection to information from that specific level of vibration. Training the consciousness to focus firmly on a level of vibration enables a clear and constant flow of information from that level. It helps us sense more clearly and interpret more accurately. This focussing helps us sense which level of vibration we are working with, and the way we connect at that level. This focussing and increased sensitivity helps us identify when we are truly in our heart-space.

One of the first stumbling blocks and causes of friction, when supporting people trying to work with, or focus on, heart-space vibration, is that they *think* they are in heart-space. *Thinking* you are somewhere means you are in mind vibration. *Thinking* heart-space and love is not *being* in heart-space and love. *Thinking* it, you are not there. *Being* it, without thought, is when you are truly there.

As a Passive Receiver, the more skilled you become at travelling your consciousness up and down the cord of light, and connecting to different energy centres and layers, the better you will become at identifying and living within heart-space vibration.

Sensitivity is key.

Sensitivity comes from identifying and living within heart-space, where we find the gate to our soul-self, love, interconnection, healing and our unique aspect of 'Is'.

As a Passive Receiver of information, we can focus on levels of vibration to become more efficient at receiving information. For example, when we work psychically or clairvoyantly, we focus on each of these levels of frequency to become more efficient at receiving and translating the information received. But this is still looking for, and receiving, information. Although the conscious movement through levels of vibration is fluid and quick, it is still single-level focus, and it is information given to us, even if we seek it.

When we are Dynamic Creators, we are multi-vibrational and multi-conscious, so we are within the flow of knowing. Therefore, truth and information are within us, rather than sought. We can still consciously focus on one specific level of vibration, but we may also be conscious of other levels of vibration at the same time.

The information just is, and the knowing within us, just is.

As a Passive Receiver we are given ideas or new fully formed 'patterns'. As a Dynamic Creator we can participate in the conscious formation of ideas or new 'patterns'. We are part of the process, rather than receiving the formed results of the process.

As a Passive Receiver, the heart-space is key. It is the door to oneself and to that which 'Is'. To connect to, or even exist within the heart-space vibration, is a massive step forward in our spiritual evolution. It is the vibration at which we sense that there is something 'more', and that we are not just physical.

When we begin to want to help others, want to grow and learn about ourselves and our truth, and want to be of service to that which 'Is', or to the world in any way at all, this is when we begin to sense heart-space. Through heart-space we sense our interconnected nature, love, healing, our soul-self, and that which 'Is'. So, through service and caring, we begin to dip in and out of heart-space vibration, and when we unconsciously sense it, we adore it, and want to experience it more. We can't explain what it is, or what we feel, but it is love, peace and inner knowing that we connect to, and this creates a tremendous sense of joy within us. This is why people care for, and do service for, others and the world. Because they sense, even if they don't understand, the difference they are making at a very deep and profound level. This is also what happens to healers. Healers love to do healing with others as it raises their vibration to the frequency of heart-space, as this is where healing emanates from. To connect to healing energy, we need to connect to our heart-space, as this is where our connection to that which 'Is' can be accessed. Healing is brought down through the cord of light from that which 'Is', and consciously directed by the healer towards the being or place which requires the healing. Healing always emanates via heart-space, from the heart-space vibration. This is where the divine light and love from that which 'Is' is accessed.

When we are in service, or a healer, our vibration is raised in to heart-space, but often this vibration is not a constant state of being. This is due to coagulations of discordant energy, or cords, holding us at the lower levels of vibration. So, we work in service or healing, raise into our heart-space, then dip down into lower levels again. This connection is intermittent. Therefore, it is imperative to work towards heart-space living. Because if we are permanently in this vibration, healing constantly emanates from us. The light from that which 'Is' flows through us, and into all things, at all times. Every thought, word, deed, and gesture, when living as this vibration, will contain healing. So, if you work in service, or as a healer, you will be putting love and healing into everything, always. Just by *being*, you are radiating love and healing.

When we do not work on ourselves and our energetic systems, to create an efficient vehicle for sharing this love and healing, we are not working to the amazing potential that we are truly capable of. Healing and service should be a way of being, not something we visit occasionally because we have touched heart-space vibration, and this has made us feel good. To work on ourselves, to live in heart-space, and to connect to and eventually integrate our soul-selves, really is the greatest gift for all. Because in heart-space we are better for everyone and everything.

When we do healing or service to feel good about ourselves, rather than to do good, this is because we are feeding our own egos. If we are doing it to 'feel good' we tether these experiences to low level mind/emotion vibration, thus keeping us at low level frequency. Therefore, the very thing we wish for, heart-space connection, will be harder to access. If we do not identify ourselves with our service or our healing actions, and let them go, we exist in heart-space frequency, and are not pulled out of it. So, be a healer and be in service, but do not define yourself by your actions, or be needy for thanks and praise, as this will pull you away from the very thing you are seeking. This pulling up and down of frequencies, as a healer, will make you less efficient than if you work on yourself and walk towards heart-space existence.

As a Passive Receiver incarnate, we constantly battle with our own physical, emotional and mental layers of existence, and battle at resolving and dissolving disharmony at these levels of our energetic system. We are constantly trying to connect with our soul-self and that which 'Is', but this is intermittent. We receive, or must search for, our spiritual information or guidance. We battle to even recognise, let alone exist within, the heart-space frequency of vibration. If we have spiritual experience, we find it hard not to hold on to it and identify ourselves with it; this is ego. We find it hard to go beyond the signposts of our experiences and recognise their pointing of us towards heart-space existence, and onward towards incarnating our soul-self, our Dynamic Creator. But we must remember we are human, and the path towards light and truth is never an easy one.... we just need to keep on walking.

It has been very curious writing this chapter. It has taken at least 20 times longer to do, and it is the one I am least satisfied with. It came together in lumps, was incoherent, needed to be reworked and reworked and reworked. I found it hard to concentrate and make sense of what it was that needed to be written. It created immense frustration within me, as I seemed to only be able to articulate parts, but not wholes. After battling and tangling with it for days I was made aware of why it was this way. Spirit had created within me a Passive Receiver single-vibrational, single-consciousness vibration. I was having to work to produce this chapter as a Passive Receiver. It was so hard, so unclear, so disjointed and so utterly frustrating. But it was good to be reminded of what a struggle it is, and how amazing and brave it is for you to begin the journey to heart-space existence. Even if you take one step, this is fantastic, and I hope, perhaps, you go on to take another...

Mel Cross

TRANSITIONING FROM PASSIVE RECEIVER TO DYNAMIC CREATOR

The practical stages of progression

There are stages of development which are practically lived as we progress on the path from living as a Passive Receiver, to incarnating our soul and living as a Dynamic Creator.

The first way: Living without a sense of that which 'Is'

This is when we sit within the identity created for us through upbringing, conditioning, society etc... this is when we function as our 'created-self'. This is existence within the lower three levels of vibration; physical, emotional, and mind. We live within the illusion that this is the sum of existence and this disconnects us from our true essential nature – our soul-self, and the light of that which 'Is', which sits at the centre of this.

When we exist within these three levels we are plagued by insecurity, emotion, ego, fear, lust, selfishness, anger, greed and tangible experiences of life. We try to satiate the longing felt within the heart-space with relationships, money, status, belongings. We do not understand why this yearning never leaves us. We are rarely satisfied and rarely at peace. We do not hear the voice of our Truth. This is the level at which we can be distracted, affected and manipulated by malevolent, or negative, aspects of spiritual existence.

The second way: Trying to connect to that which 'Is' through action and thought

This is when we begin to live with a sense of that which 'Is' and begin to sense the light of that which 'Is' within us. The cord of connection from the light of that which 'Is' begins to tug. It is felt within your spirit-self, which connects you up to the light within your soul, and up through every level of vibration to connect to that which 'Is'. The pull of pure love, and pure light, is along this connection. It tugs in order to be noticed.

At this stage, when we begin to sense a tug within the heart-space, we begin to search for teachings at an intellectual level, and we try to understand. We search for teachers, gurus and books to try to make sense of the 'tug', and we try to do all of this within the mind at a fact-based level. Finding answers to explain the 'tug' is an intellectual exercise here. Neither the Truth, nor that which 'Is', can truly be understood within the mind.

We know it is also good to connect to others and help, so we do service, or what we believe to be 'Gods' work. We begin to look at *we* even though we still exist as *me*. We know it is essential for humans to help and nurture each other, and we know it is imperative that we care for the creations of that which 'Is', the earth, animals, plants, ecosystems etc... Through working in service, glimpses of connection may be experienced, but they are often still tethered to the lower three levels of vibration; physical, emotional and mind. Whilst our sense of duty, our service and our experiences are tethered to our false sense of 'self', our self-created identity, and our ego, growth and connection will be compromised. Helping others helps us to connect to heart-space, which is where we begin to experience our soul-self, love, healing, our interconnected nature and that which 'Is', which makes us feel great. But if we define ourselves by our service, or feel we are somehow worthier than others by our actions, we are feeding our ego, and this tethers us to low-level vibration, which pulls us back out of heart-space.

If we work in service we must do so in true humility, true love and true light, with no need for praise, recognition or thanks. It is nice to be appreciated, of course, but it is not our primary motivator for the work we do. When we work in this way it helps us connect to, and exist within, the vibration of heart-space, and will strengthen our connection to that which 'Is'. If we work to connect to the love and light of that which 'Is', and to sit within the vibration of heart-space, this is wonderful, we will grow and begin to spiritually evolve. If we work for praise, recognition or superiority, the potential to raise into higher vibration and spiritual connection will be tethered to low-level vibration. Here soul connection and connection to that which 'Is' will not be truly experienced, and our spiritual evolution will be hindered.

This is where we begin to grasp the concept of the duality of the process. We must experience and then let go of the experience. We must understand and not understand. We must know and then not know. We must *do* and *be*.

The third way: Trying to connect to that which 'Is' through contemplation

Here we begin to understand that withdrawing from the physical, emotional and mind, helps us move towards the next level of vibration – the 'heart-space' level. Within our heart-space we find our Truth and our connection to that which 'Is'. We may not fully understand what heart-space is, but here we begin to recognise it more consciously, and sense its authenticity. When we pull our consciousness to this level of vibration, we are now able to sense the truth of our soul, our connection to the light of that which 'Is', unconditional love, healing, and the interconnectedness of all things. We know we are one facet of the whole, and what we do, think, say and feel affects the *all*. We begin to sense *we* instead of *me*.

The more we can consciously sit within this space, the stronger it will be felt. This is the space of contemplative existence. If we pull all emotions and thoughts into this space, we begin to sense the difference between our 'created-self' and our true soul-self. Our understanding of, and reactions to, our thoughts and emotions, can be very different when they are experienced within the heart-space; we observe them rather than be consumed by them. There is a greater sense of 'Truth,' and solutions to previously perceived insurmountable problems can be resolved whilst within this space.

Our life just begins to make more sense. Not in the head, but in the heart.

Although deprivation of physical, emotional and mind stimulus can put one in a state of isolation and receptivity, it is perceived that this often cannot be achieved in ordinary life, it must be done in separation. But this is not actually true. This connection can be nurtured and taught through understanding the energetic/vibrational layers of existence, so that we can exist within it in everyday life, not just within meditation and prayer. This is existing within heart-space, and the energy in which we exist will be disseminated vibrationally to others. Living in heart-space affects everyone and everything around us. This is where instead of reaching *upward* to connect to that which 'Is', we reach *inward*, and begin to bring the vibration of that which 'Is' here for all.

When sitting within heart-space, all physical, emotional and mental processes can be examined and worked with, practically and energetically, to clear, cleanse and reveal the truth of our soul; our true-self. This process can also be taught. It is the process of stripping away to reveal our true light within.

As the lower levels are dissolved this creates fluidity of movement of energy between these layers and allows the light within spirit-self heart-space to begin to consciously connect to the light within the centre of soul.

The fourth way: Existing as both spirit-self and soul-self incarnate

This is when we are consciously existing within heart-space, and occasionally dropping out of it, rather than existing below heart-space and occasionally raising up into it. This is existing within the meditative vibration, not in an altered state of consciousness, but in an altered state of vibration. We are still fully functioning and participating in life, but from a raised, heart-space vibration.

When enough space within our energy system has been created by dissolving solidified feelings, emotions, thoughts, physical issues, and programming, heart-space expands and a *conscious* connection between spirit-self and soul-self is made, via the cord of that which 'Is' which flows in connection between them.

In this intermediate stage, we exist with both single-level vibrational spirit-self and multi-vibrational soul. We have incarnated in part our soul-self, but we still have some single vibrational outer layers. These are the heart-space level, communication level, spiritual level and level of that which 'Is'.

We need to process things through this intermediary level, as going from single-level vibrational Passive Receiver to multi-vibrational

Dynamic Creator in one go would be too extreme for one's energetic system, and our capacity to process and embody this new way of existence would also be too extreme. Therefore, it is embodied in stages for energetic, emotional and mental adjustment to take place.

This intermediary stage is also important for conscious single-layered connection to be accessed, so that we can seek information that teaches us how to embody this new way of existing, and so that we can be taught how to work with and take care of this energy. In this way we can still seek guidance from spiritual sources as we have done before.

As we now have multi-vibrational soul partially existing within these levels, without the blockages of physical, emotional and mind levels, we are now able to work with and experience much greater degrees of spiritual experience and have a much greater sensitivity to energetic harmony and disharmony. We still 'receive' information from spirit, but we also are learning to exist as a multi-vibrational soul-self, and experience more easily the free-flowing dynamic creative aspect of that which 'Is'. We are learning to be within the flow of knowing.

This transitioning is a very hectic time for spiritual experience. We sense so much more, are more sensitive, and are sometimes bombarded with experiences and information. We need to keep a steady pace and maintain a level head. This can be the time that we become egoic due to our incredible experiences and new-found knowledge. This is when we can be pulled down into mind and emotion vibration, as we can be lured into the shackles of our own self-importance and perceived superiority. This is actually a good thing. If we are not able to keep to the path of love, faith, trust, truth, surrender, stillness and humility, we will not access the totality of our soul, and our soul-self will not fully incarnate. Soul-self must only fully incarnate when we are a pure enough vessel to house it, and our intent is within pure love and light. This is where surrendering to the process and humility keep us true.

As this transition takes place there will be physical, emotional, mental and spiritual disharmony which comes and goes through this process at every level. Usually when we are closest to moving through to the next stage of the process the tests, darkness and utter hopelessness will be felt the most and strongest. These challenges are presented to us to ensure we are fully focused on that which 'Is', to test our faith, our trust, and our ability to totally surrender to the process. We need to be able to live to these principles for soul-self to live comfortably when incarnated. We need to be able to return to, and live within, these ideals no matter what. If we can remember that the more painful it gets, the closer we are to growth and change, all we need to do is just keep on walking. These dark times are to identify and illuminate those who truly have trust. If you truly walk in love, faith, trust, truth, surrender, stillness and humility you will move through these times. Anyone who does not walk immersed in the totality of these ways will not access their true potential. This is because the enormity of their potential, if used for anything other than sharing light, love and understanding, would be immensely problematic. This also keeps the discordancy of incarnate experience from causing discomfort or damage to the perfection of the soul.

The fifth way: Existing as soul-self; becoming ready to facilitate that which 'Is' to incarnate through us, in this lifetime

Once spirit-self and soul-self are consciously connected and freely flowing, soul-self can be brought down into expanded heart-space and incarnate in its fullest sense. For this to take place we must be existing in love, faith, trust, truth, surrender, stillness and humility. This is when our spirit-self integrates back into soul-self, and soul-self is pulled down within us via the cord of light connecting us to that which 'Is' above. Our own unique soul-self, and our own unique aspect of that which 'Is', now resides within us.

This is the level at which our soul has fully incarnated into our energetic system and our bandwidth has been raised to the levels of love/healing, communication and spiritual connection. We have dissolved our three lower levels of vibration, and our consciousness now fluidly connects in a multi-conscious way within all levels of vibration.

Although we now function in a multi-vibrational way, our energy field has reversed through the pulling up of spirit-self and the pulling down of soul-self. As spirit-self the physical layer of vibration is closest to the physical body. As soul the physical level of vibration is furthest away from our physical body in our energy field.

Although we are multi-conscious within all levels of vibration, we experience only that which we can comprehend within our human understanding, with the restrictions of our human brain. That which we are not able to comprehend we sense as flowing knowing. We do not need to understand all within the mind, because we sense all within our soul. It needs no explanation, comprehension or understanding. We just *know*, and within this knowing, all is harmoniously peaceful. We sense our connection to *All*.

We exist at heart-space frequency as a multi-vibrational, multi-conscious, multi-connected, Dynamic Creator soul and we work from a point of Truth. Both our truth and the truth of that which 'Is'. Our connection to the highest level of vibration – Divine 'Is', has strengthened, and our capacity to interpret and share information has increased. We shine brightly, and our light and raised vibration affects everything around us. Just by *being* we are making the world a better, purer and more beautiful place. We are the stars guiding people in the darkness. This is when we work to exist as an 'Is'-being within the human being experience.

When we constantly work at this vibration, in love, faith, trust, truth, surrender, stillness and humility, and show ourselves to be a pure vessel for carrying the divine light of that which 'Is' (highest vibration light and love), that which 'Is' (highest vibration light and love) may choose to incarnate within you, and a two-way communicating connection is made. This gift is a state of enlightenment/illumination. We cannot force this gift and cannot chase this gift. Enlightenment/illumination is a gift from that which 'Is', whose light blossoms within us, and our light blossoms within it, only when we are truly ready.

Mel Cross

AWAKENING AND ENLIGHTENMENT

The difference

There needs to be a clearer understanding of the terms 'awakening' and 'enlightenment', as these are being owned and tethered to an individual's ego and need for superiority amongst his or her peers, or likeminded individuals. And, as we have spoken about already, we need to understand the importance of not owning, labelling or tethering experiences to create an identity, as this has a negative effect on one's progression towards the state of full-soul integration.

Firstly, for the purposes of explanation and clarity, I am using the word 'Enlightenment'. This word could be 'Illumination', 'Light-filled', or any similar description. Words can cause disharmony and misunderstanding, as we have discussed before. So, I have used 'Enlightenment', as this seems to be the common parlance at this present time, for the description of one who has become fully aware, in a full state of being, but with the 'Is'-given addition of being 'Is'/light-filled. One who has moved beyond soul-integration, to exist as full 'Is'-being.

When an individual is gently shaken awake or dramatically slapped awake from the slumbering sleepwalk of life, into a state of awakened existence, there are many effects felt both physically, emotionally, mentally and spiritually. These are all signposts and pointers towards the true-path, the path towards heart-space existence and full soul-integration. These effects and experiences are not, in and of themselves, 'enlightenment'. They are effects of the awakening process. 'Enlightenment', in its truest sense, is a very different thing indeed.

The beginning of the awakening process is usually made known to an individual by a subtle or dramatic spiritual experience. This comes in many shapes and forms, from suddenly seeing auras, being able to heal, seeing angels, hearing spirit, connecting to a guide, for example. It can be life-changing and profound at the deepest level. This experience and subsequent experiences are all effects of the awakening process, and are signposts pointing us on our path towards heart-space existence, and soul-integration. This is not being 'Enlightened' in its truest sense, these are signs that you are being awakened, and that you may begin to experience 'enlightened thinking'. The phrase 'enlightened thinking' means that you will begin to think outside of conventional parameters, and beyond conventional understanding. This is all fantastic. Enlightened thinking shows you are now able to begin walking the path. It shows you that the three lower-levels of vibration are beginning to be disrupted, and space for a more fluid connection to dynamic, creative that which 'Is' is being felt. These are the first stirrings of communication with your soul from which comes clarity and 'truth' in understanding and thought. It comes from the stronger spiritual connection which is part of the awakening process, as you can receive and interpret information given to you via guides, spirit and 'connected' experience; from the intermittent spirit-self/soul connection, where *truth* and understanding are received and understood.

Spiritual experience, and unconstrained enlightened thought, are incredible, overwhelming and beyond explanation regarding how amazing one can feel when beginning to experience such things. But this is not true enlightenment. This is the crucial time when individuals can become lost or caught within these experiences. It is so elating and so overwhelming that one wants to experience these more and more. But this is not the way. Spiritual experience is a side-effect of walking the path to, or as, Dynamic Creator.

If you truly walk the path your spiritual experiences will increase as a matter of course. If you focus on the spiritual experience, and take your eye away from the path, you will become lost, and your progression will be halted. This is due to one focussing on the spiritual experience, defining oneself by it, and owning it. By doing this you are tethering these experiences to the low-level vibrations of mind and emotion, as you are using them to define your created-self. Your progression, when your created-self is defined by these experiences, will be stifled. This is also the case with using the phrase 'I've been enlightened,' when what you have felt are overwhelming spiritual experiences, and/or understanding outside of conventional, restrained thinking via the movement of dynamic, creative 'Is'.

Spiritual experience is not highest vibrational *'Is'* experience; they are very different.

In spiritual communities the 'I've been enlightened' phrase is bandied about quite freely. But this is not because true enlightenment has taken place, it is because one has tethered this new understanding and experience to one's identity, thus creating feelings of superiority, resulting in an inflated ego. This holds an individual within low-level vibrations of created-self and halts one's progression on the path.

Those who *claim*, rather than *exist* at, a state of enlightenment, are false.

Those who say they have enlightened thinking, with humility, respect, wisdom, love, surrender and awe, without claim, superiority or ego, are truly enlightened thinkers working with dynamic, creative 'Is'. These are the individuals who experience true enlightened thought, increasing spiritual experience, and who are truly walking the path.

These individuals will lead humanity forward.

'Enlightenment', in its truest sense, is profound and beyond definition, but I will try in some clumsy way, for the purposes of understanding.

'Enlightenment' is a state of total communion with that which 'Is'.

The unity in one body of receptive 'Is' at the centre of your soul – love, the dynamic, creative 'Is' flowing with truth, and the above 'light' of highest vibrational 'Is', all shining together.

When the three truly become One, within.

It is a state reached after heart-space existence, and after full soul-integration.

In the evolutionary process, spirit-self reintegrates with soul, and soul becomes fully incarnate in this lifetime. With Enlightenment, soul reintegrates with 'Is', and 'Is' becomes incarnate within you, in this lifetime. But this state of divine being is not your choice.

Through love, faith, trust, truth, surrender, stillness and humility, we walk the path towards soul-integration, and once this is achieved we continue, but, rather than walking the path in this way, we learn to exist and *be* in this way. Through total dedication to 'Is' in every moment, thought and deed, and through love, faith, trust, truth, humility, stillness and surrender as our way of continued *being*, we create a perfect vehicle for 'Is' to inhabit more fully, just as we created the perfect vehicle for true-soul to inhabit fully.

Whether 'Is' integrates fully with us is not our choice.

It is for us to keep focus on the light, walk in dedication, and wait.

When people walk the path towards soul-self, or are living as soul-self, they will experience flashes of 'Is' experience. This is VERY different to spiritual experience.
Spiritual experiences can be profound and life-changing, and are often mistaken for 'Is' experiences, but they are not the same.

Spiritual experiences are created from 'Is', but are not 'Is'.

'Is' experience is profound and at a deeper soul level. The love, light and intensity of an 'Is' experience cannot be explained, it can only be experienced.

Our connection to 'Is' becomes stronger as we walk the path, exist in heart-space, and move towards soul-integration.

Spiritual experience points the direction,
'Is' experience keeps us walking.

Once 'Is' has been felt, the sometimes-excruciating experiences and tests given whilst walking the path will be embraced with joy, if it means the connection to this profound state is touched again. 'Is' experience keeps us walking the path, always.

The state of 'Enlightenment' is gifted upon you when you are at a pure state of being and dedication. The light of that which 'Is' will enter you, and you will enter that which 'Is'. There are no further words.

Enlightenment is a state of pure light *being* and pure light *consciousness*.

If you meet someone in an enlightened state you will see it, feel it, and know it, often without words; and to come across this is rare. Should you be gifted with such an acquaintance listen, learn, observe and absorb.

There have been enlightened individuals throughout history, and they are the pioneers, the awakeners, the illuminators. Some are gifted this in their lifetime, and some are born in this purest state of divinity. Each one a blessing beyond our human comprehension. Never forget this.

So, when you come across the self-proclaimed or pondering 'enlightened', you may have come across an egoic spiritual experiencer, or enlightened thinker. Or, if you are incredibly lucky, you may one-day meet, or become, a truly enlightened individual. If you meet one, they will be the one who makes no claims; look deep into their eyes, and the truth of their being will shine. This is when you know.

Enlightenment Is.

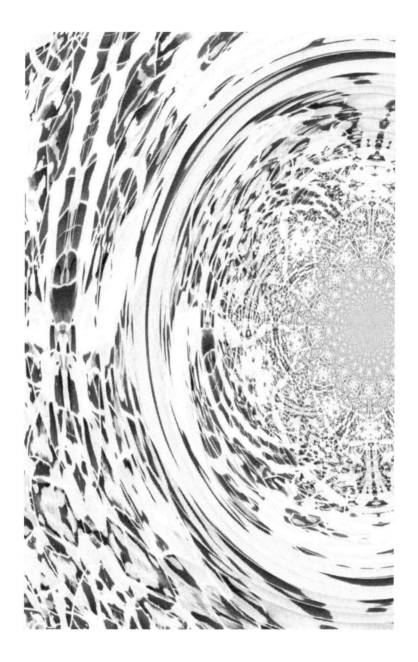

PRINCIPLES OF CONNECTION

Supporting, aligning and maintaining your Cord of Light

There are essential qualities to be worked upon which will help you to identify, align with, and strengthen, your cord of light. The cord of light is essential when journeying towards connecting to your soul and that which 'Is'. It is also an integral part of process when working towards becoming a Dynamic Creator.

As words can be misunderstood, or misinterpreted, I will try to define these qualities to bring greater understanding. This understanding will assist you when walking your path towards your own truth, and the truth of that which 'Is'. These qualities, when consciously connected to and lived, will keep your cord of light aligned and flowing.

The first of these qualities is:

Love

Love. The most important tool of all; in all things and in all ways. If it is the only quality we choose to work with, let it be so. After all, love is the answer to all things, is in all things, and is all things.

When we talk of everyday 'love' we often use it in our human understanding of relationship love or use it to describe that which brings us pleasure. That which we 'like', 'desire' or 'need'. In a human context, 'love', or our misperceived idea of what love is, is what we try to identify with, and use, for us to connect to that which 'Is'.

'God is Love' we hear, so we try to connect to God with our human experience and understanding of love. But our 'mind' and 'emotional' experience of love is based on our created-selves experience of human love. Human love is often needy, and almost always conditional. We love things or people whilst they bring us pleasure or fulfil our needs. Once this pleasure has gone, or that which we love no longer fulfils our needs, the love wanes and dies. This is not the love I speak of in this text.

We use the word love to define that which we like or admire. This is not the definition of love used in this text.

We use the word love to describe that which we desire. We love a person because they fulfil a need in oneself; whatever that need is. Be it physical, emotional or mental. But it is almost always conditional. People always say it is unconditional, but it isn't. There are almost always conditions which will diminish the love, and always situations which will shatter this love. This is also not the love I speak of in this text.

Sometimes we come across love which almost fulfils a need within oneself. A love which touches one's heart or helps soothe the pain and longing felt within oneself. Often, we identify and fill the pain and longing we feel with human things we love and relationships, but this never totally satiates the longing. Of course, 'Is' 'love' runs through all things, within all things, and is part of all things. Other people can bring out the deepest of love within us, and they can unlock the doors to that deeper divine love. They can teach us, show us, and reflect back at us. Our human relationship love can indeed feel divine. If it does truly feel divine it is because we are in the flow of the divine with that other, without constriction, restriction or condition. It is pure and flowing between you both. Together you have gone beyond human love in to heart-space vibration – the place of 'Is' love. In this instance, the relationship you have will contain the essential core or true 'love', the love I talk of in this text.

So, let me explain.

Love.
Love is.
Love is All.
Love is in.
Love is around.
Love is through.
Love is the life and flowing nature of that which 'Is'.

Love within, is our own unique aspect of the divine 'Is', which shines brightly at our very core.

Love around, is the dynamic, creative love of that which 'Is'. It is the flow of love from that which was, that which is, and that which will be. It is the love from which all things come and to which all things will return.

Love through, is the connection to that which 'Is' above, which floods us, and everything in existence, with light and love, ALWAYS.

The love we connect to when we live within our heart-space, is via our connecting cord to that which 'Is', the source of all love. This is when we truly sense, truly know and truly experience the love for us from that which 'Is'. This is the connection to love we seek. This is the love that we wish to be, in every thought, word, and deed, each and every day. This is the love we want to live within, every second of every day.

And it is the love we wish to share, as a conduit for that which 'Is'.

Through us love reaches all people, all creatures, all plants, all elements, all things. This love works through us, to connect to all things, to be shared with all things, unconditionally – always. This love, if we look clearly, if we listen carefully, and if we truly *feel* with our heart and soul, can be found everywhere, in all things, always. It is the love we feel for every atom, of everything, both seen and unseen.

This love is the divine flow of love and light from that which 'Is', which reaches and is consciously heard by our soul. It awakens us, illuminates us, guides us, holds us, speaks to us, is shared by us, satiates us, and flows freely through us and holds our hands and hearts through all things; ALWAYS.

This love is the fire in our soul which keeps us walking – regardless.

Faith

Faith is the inner knowing and personal connection from our soul to that which 'Is'. It is the knowing, at a profound level, that that which 'Is' is within, around and through us. It is the *knowing* of that which 'Is'. Faith is intangible and indescribable, but it is the thing that holds our mind, body, heart and soul in the knowing of that which 'Is' and love. Faith is our sense of connection to the infinite love and light of that which 'Is'. It is the felt presence of the existence of the cord of light. Faith is in our knowing, and that knowing cannot be felt in the emotions or the mind. Faith is felt within the heart-space. Faith is our sense of connection to that which 'Is'. It is what we focus on, and hold tightly to, when all is shaking. It is what pulls us up and pulls us through all things.

Faith comes from sensing and experiencing the cord of light which connects us from the spark within our heart-space to that which 'Is'. Faith is the cord of light which holds us and nourishes us. Through it comes our connection to divine love and light from that which 'Is'. Faith holds us always, and we hold on to it. It cannot be fully articulated, shown or proved, but in our knowing, we sense its presence.

Trust

Trust is what we must have for faith to flow that which 'Is' into our lives. We must trust that all will be well, for faith to do this. Trust is what we need when all around us is in chaos, does not make sense, or does not go as we had planned. Trust is what is required by us to know all is as it should be, even when it does not seem that way, and that all, in the end will be well. Trust is what we need for us to receive guidance. The guidance comes to us because we have faith, but trust is what allows this to manifest.

Trust is faith in action.

It is faith which connects us to that which gives us inner knowing, and we must learn to trust this. Sensing that which 'Is' guides us, supports us, informs us, loves us and lights our way is faith. Trust is knowing this will manifest in our lives.

We must never let go of faith, and we must always try to trust, no matter how hard things are or how dark things get. Faith and trust enable us to walk, even when the path has disappeared, or we are lost, or we are weak. Faith and trust hold one hand each and walk with us and guide us – always.

Truth

Truth is felt within the heart-space. Truth is not known in the head. Truth is our inner guidance from that which 'Is'. Truth is not facts – truth is our sense of knowing. Truth is transient, ever-flowing, movable, changeable and difficult (as all these things are!) to fully articulate. Truth is inner knowing within the heart-space, and is from the moment by moment flowing, dynamic, creative aspect of that which 'Is'. The truth can change, moment by moment, therefore the truth can only be sensed in the present.

Truth may vary in its translation from person to person, but ultimately Truth is divine, all-encompassing and all pervading. It is

Mel Cross

divine truth, eternal truth, fundamental truth. It is guidance, it is the underpinning essence within all beliefs, and apart from all beliefs, and it is illumination. Truth is felt in the heart and often questioned in the head. It is not intellectual, it is *knowing*. It is felt, rather than thought. If it is captured and rationalised and placed within the confines of our created-self, or our physical, emotional or mental circumstance, it will be misconstrued, misinterpreted and compromised.

Truth is received from love, via faith, in trust and manifests in our heart-space. It is of the moment and always in the present. It should not be referred back to or gathered in anticipation for what is to come. It is connection to all that 'Is', in the present moment, and is ever-flowing, and ever-changing.

Truth ensures our footsteps move in the right way, at the right time, in the right direction. Truth cannot be dictated by others, it comes purely from that which 'Is', and is sensed within the heart-space.

From love (that which 'Is'), through faith, in trust, we receive Truth.

Surrender

As human beings, we try to control and steer our lives and circumstances. By doing so we create what we want, and what we believe is to our best benefit. We try to create forms of physical, emotional and mental safety and security in a way we perceive to be right for us. But, we drive, order and create our lives, with physical, emotional and mental direction, according to what our created-self thinks is best. And, we now understand, created-self rarely knows best. Knowing always comes from soul-self, rather than Passive Receiver created-self, and that knowing originates from divine, creative, that which 'Is', and that which 'Is' of pure vibration; the constant emanator of love and light.

Created/spirit-self is not capable of directing the soul and that which 'Is', so that which 'Is' always guides us the right way, even when we do not understand the right way, or the right way seems wrong and excruciatingly painful. When we fight against the flow of Truth, or try

136

to direct it, change it, or *think* we know better, we cause ourselves unnecessary pain and delay in the path of our lives.

If we accept that love, via faith, through trust, comes truth, and we surrender to the divine flow of Truth, we suddenly become a part of the flow of the divine. We no longer struggle, fight, or drown, in the flow of our life. The key is to totally trust that which 'Is', hold up our hands and surrender to the process. The process, when flowing, is clear, pure, and of love and light. These waves of love, light, and truth, flow through us, around us and in us. They guide, direct, enlighten and hold us, as we surrender within faith.

When we put barriers, blocks, thoughts, feelings, and all manner of created-self debris in the way, to control our lives in an 'I know best' kind of way, we create diversions, blocks and hinder our own serene flow of that which 'Is'. When we surrender, we grow, learn and thrive. This is not to say we are weak or passive in any way. Indeed, again, it is a pile of contradictions. Surrender takes faith and trust in the flow of truth, from love. It takes a strong and willing heart to hand all into the heart of love and light to navigate the sea of life. It does not mean we do not strive or take responsibility for our lives and actions; we do. We strive to grow, to learn, to trust, to love, to live, and to be the best that we possibly can. But when we become stuck, lost, or out of the flow, instead of struggling we should surrender. When we feel we are at the end of the line, cannot move forward, or are fearful, desperate, scared or in pain, it is then that we truly surrender. When we can take no more, when the outlook is bleak, or the darkness too blinding, it is here, in the greatest act, we truly put our faith and trust in that which 'Is'. We stop fighting and float in the flow, rather than fighting against the tide.

It is not giving up, it is offering our situation up to that which 'Is', to carry and guide us.

It is in this surrender, in total faith and love, that we flow to the right place, the right time, the right thing. It may not be what or how we thought it would be, but eventually we realise that in this act, that which 'Is' has held us, guided us, soothed us and washed us up upon the shore. And we have washed up in one piece, with clearer eyes, a larger heart, and a fist-full of knowing.

Flowing through pain and suffering, rather than fighting it, is one of the best providers of connection, growth and understanding.

Surrender is incredibly hard, and beautiful in its simplicity. It is contradictorily perfect.

Stillness

Once we have learned to surrender to and within the flow, we need to create circumstances to recognise, listen to, and consciously inhabit this movement and stillness.

Stillness is the point of perfect balance and is the centre of all things. It is the moment poised delicately between movement. If we do not make time to find stillness, in order to be within silence, we are not taking the time, nor making the effort, to hear the wisdom of truth which can be heard within this, which is received within the heart. We need to clear space for new patterns to pour forth, and to listen. If we do not sit within silence, we are less discerning and less receptive to the clear sensing of the love and light which flows within the stillness. That which 'Is' resides within the movement and the stillness, within the words and within the silence; the perfect moment, within and between these things is the place of perfect connection to everything and nothing.

The silence within stillness can be found at the centre of most contemplative, creative and movement practices. It is entering stillness to find 'flow' or entering 'flow' to find stillness.

In a prayerful space we flow words up the cord of light to that which 'Is'. When we are in contemplative space we listen to the flow of creative non-verbal wisdom within the silence. This up and down flow, within stillness and silence, strengthens the connection to that which 'Is' and strengthens the flow within this connection. The stillness at the centre of the cord is the connection from that which 'Is', highest vibration of Love and light, to receptive that which 'Is' at the centre of our soul. Around and through which, is the flowing dynamic, creative, no-thing that which 'Is'.

It can be found in the centre of the stillness of contemplation/meditation; when one does not pull to the left or to the right. Not towards anything or away from anything. To identify perfectly with everything and nothing; to be both and neither. We push nothing away and pull nothing towards us; we just 'be'. It is a place of balance and centring.

This space, at the centre point of creativity, is the silent stillness within the flow of the movement of the creative process. This space is also the place of stillness and silence within the centre point of physical movement practices. When we are in flow with the movement of the body, we reach the stillness and silence within this.

The stillness and silence within the flowing cord of light is the stillness and silence beyond and within the movement of the physical, beyond and within the movement of emotions and beyond and within the movement of thoughts. Once we have surrendered, stillness is the place of listening, so we can recognise and hear truth. Once we do this, we can bring this listening and truth into our everyday lives.

Humility

Humility can be interpreted and understood in different ways. People often believe that being humble and walking in humility is a way of connecting to, respecting, or creating a sense of 'lower than' or 'less than'. To forgo our ego to create lowly. But if this state of humility is created by mind and conscious intent, it can often be counterproductive and inauthentic. When we create ourselves a state of 'less than', and *act* in 'humility', it can sometimes be used as a statement of 'lowly = closer to God'. When we create this state in falseness we are, in fact, acting from ego. If we are 'less than' we are creating a state of believing that we are 'more than', or 'better than', those who are not humble. This worthiness comes from ego, and ego is from mind. Mind is a low-level frequency which sits underneath the heart-space level of vibration. The heart-space vibration is not *lower than* but is, in fact, *higher than* mind-created humility. When we raise above mind-created humility to true humility, in the sense which I write of in this text, it is from heart-space vibration. Humility is of the heart and love, not of the mind and thought.

This humility is not about being 'less than' and putting ourselves lower than others and that which 'Is', to be respectful or connected (although respectful and connected are vital, of course). The humility I talk of is recognising our own unique aspect of the divine and being the best and greatest incarnation of this that we can. When we do this, we sit within heart-space. When we sit within heart-space we are in true and fluid connection to our true soul-self and the indescribable wonder of that which 'Is'. When we sit within our truth, and the triple aspect nature of that which 'Is', we can be nothing other than truly humble. The greatness, beauty, light, love and infinite and indescribable nature of that which 'Is', once truly experienced, leaves you in no other state than humility. This is when we recognise we are not the centre of our Universe, but we are a tiny and beautiful part of it, as is everyone else.

When we experience and understand we are an infinitely tiny aspect of something so divine and so incredible – this is when we feel humility.

When we recognise our light, which sits at the centre of our soul – this is when we feel humility.

When we experience the flow of that which 'Is' moving through us, and recognise we are connected to, and in communication with, that which 'Is', and all things that were, are, and will be – this is when we understand humility.

When we recognise we are part of the incredible 'Is', we can be nothing more nor less than in total wonder and total humility.

Humility is not a consciously created way of being or living. Humility is a natural state we obtain when we live within our heart-space and begin to truly experience the indescribable nature of that which 'Is'. If we do not brag and do not become ego from this experience, and when we use it for good and share it, rather than covet or keep it to ourselves, we maintain our humility. If we grade ourselves, or define ourselves, by our spiritual experience or worthy actions, we move out of heart-space, and out of true humility.

When we walk in true humility it can create a sense of grace when helping others. It can inspire us to help people from all walks of life. It can lead us to a life of service or doing 'God's work'. It can also help us to lead a simple, unadorned, unmaterialistic, non-egoic life. It can lead us to give up many practical aspects of our lives, relationships, or emotional ties, to walk our path in simplicity. It can lead us to live a very humble life indeed. A simple life lived because of the humility experienced within the heart-space is an outward projection of an inward state of uncomplicated being, and an expression of total love for that which 'Is' in every way we can show it.

A humble life is an expression of the energetic stripping back and dissolving of that which defines us as our created-self, and that which stops us connecting to the true nature of our soul. Simplicity in our lives is an expression of the clarity we require in our energetic system (physical, emotional and mind). The same clarity that we need to achieve in order for us to connect to our soul and that which 'Is'.

To live an uncomplicated life from a point of wonder and awe of that which 'Is', is living a humble life with humility.

If we begin by living a simple life, in service, without need or complication, it may lead us to experience humility within the heart-space. By giving up the materialistic, egoic life it may raise us into heart-space frequency, which will enable us to embrace humility in the 'awe' sense. This may indeed help us with our progression towards conscious connection to that which 'Is', but when we force humility it is from ego, and ego is low-level vibration of the mind. If it is forced, it is inauthentic. If it is forced it is not 'surrendering', and it is not from a point of connection to Truth, and being able to listen to our truth and the truth of that which 'Is'.

Humility is wonder in surrender.

Humility is not about unworthiness and insignificance. Humility is about recognising, and being in awe and wonder of, the greatness, vastness and indescribable, overwhelming, infinite, beauty and love of that which 'Is'. It is not about how lesser we are – it is truly about recognition of, thanks for, and love of, that which 'Is'. The joy and ecstatic love of recognising we are a tiny part of something so utterly vast and wonderful, is when we experience true humility. Humility is thanks, wonder and joy, at our tiny part in such a magnificent whole. Humility is not about recognising how lowly we are. Humility is about recognising the greatness of that which 'Is'.

Humility is the anchor which must be deeply cast in order to facilitate that which 'Is' to pull down and incarnate into every aspect of our lives. We must strive upwards to meet that which 'Is', and humility helps that which 'Is' to pull downwards to meet us.

Gratitude

Gratitude is giving thanks, and we must remember to be thankful for all things and all experiences; always. Deep and humble gratitude for our lives and for that which 'Is'. No matter how good or how bad life is, no matter if we are lost, lonely, sad, or happy, we must always walk in gratitude. Not blame, not anger, not hatred, but gratitude for all things, at all times.

Life is always as it should be and guiding us the right way, no matter what the situation or how we feel about it. We must give thanks for the experiences we have, the guidance given, and the lessons learned; both in the bad times as well as the good. Our life is a precious gift and every part of it requires gratitude.

When we walk with humility, deepest gratitude comes as a part of this.

Gratitude always.

The path

The path towards heart-space, living in heart-space, dissolving our created-self and experiences, connecting to our soul and that which 'Is', and bringing our soul to incarnate in this lifetime, is brought through the qualities discussed in this chapter. Love, faith, trust, truth, surrender, stillness and humility, with gratitude running through all of these.

If we apply these qualities in all we do and think, always, we will forever be moving forward with the correct guidance towards our soul-self and that which 'Is'. These qualities, when applied, will assist us every step of the way.

When we walk in faith and truly strive to do the work of that which 'Is', we work with these. They are essential in all aspects of everything we do when we walk towards our connection to that which 'Is', and our connection to our true soul-self.

Although these qualities are used at different times and often out of sequence, they do, in fact, form a very strong chained link from us to that which 'Is'.

'Love' is that which 'Is'. In all its magnificence and light. We connect to love with faith.

Faith is the sensed link to that which 'Is' and *knowing* of that which 'Is'. It does exist as the cord of light which connects us to that which 'Is'.

Trust is faith in a practical sense. From love through faith, trust brings love into our lives. This practical application of love is what connects us to 'Truth'.

Truth guides us. This truth is *knowing* from your soul and the dynamic, creative flow of that which 'Is'.

To apply that knowing and truth to guide and support us we must, on occasion, surrender to the process, or surrender trying to control the process. In this surrender we truly act in trust and faith. Surrendering often brings great change and growth. Once we have surrendered we need to create stillness within us, and within the flow of silence, so that we can listen to the truth which can now be heard. We now become aware of that which 'Is', our soul, and the incredible process we are part of. This is when we become humble in the wonder of that which 'Is', and our unique divine aspect of that which 'Is'. Humility keeps us grounded, in awe, and encourages us to become more connected and a better conduit or vehicle for that which 'Is'.

And gratitude in all things and for all things, helps us be thankful for our journey, wherever it leads, and no matter how good or bad the path is that we travel. Gratitude for the gift of life that that which 'Is' has blessed us with, supports us in, and guides us through. There is so much to be thankful for.

Sometimes the journey we undertake to achieve a stronger and stronger connection to our soul and that which 'Is' can be terrifying, painful, confusing, contradictory or overwhelming, *but* there is one important thread which must run through all of this.

And that thread is joy!

We must remember this always. Sometimes our journey seems so intense and so serious we forget joy, we forget to have fun, we forget to laugh. We forget to throw caution to the wind and throw ourselves whole-heartedly in to this incredible gift of our life. We have not been given life to be sad, to be in pain, or as some sort of punishment. We have been blessed with a unique aspect of that which 'Is' at our very core, to explore, to embrace our uniqueness, and at the same time celebrate our unity with the collective whole of life on the planet. We should laugh, dance, sing, play and explore. We should celebrate our bodies and our minds as the gifts of expression and experience that they are. We should enjoy things!

And that joy is also a celebration of our part of, and connection to, that which 'Is'. Joy is in us, through us and around us. It should be radiating and shared authentically.

Joy and love always.

Life should be fun. In the small and the big things.

We are incredibly lucky, so let's celebrate this, always.

Mel Cross

HEART-SPACE

Love energy

Before there was time, physical existence, and matter, there was Love. This moved through all, around all, and was part of all; as it is now and how it always will be. Love is.

We as human beings are a physical manifestation of that ever-present love. We are the incarnation of that love into physical form. But we are conditioned and manipulated to believe that we are not a being of love, that we are only our physical, emotional, and mind selves. We become the illusion that this is all that we are, that this is all that exists. We become veiled from our unique divine facet of love, and that veiled facet is found within our heart-space, at the centre of our soul.

As humans, we find ourselves on the never-ending search to 'find ourselves', to find 'love', to connect to our spiritual nature, and to consciously connect to and build a relationship with that which 'Is'. We travel, we read, we find teachers, and we search and search, but the answers to all our questions, and our lifetime of searching, resides within us; within our heart-space. We already have everything we require to find peace, love, interconnection to all, and connection to that which 'Is'. It is in this space where we also find our truth, and our true soul-self. It is here where our relationship with that which 'Is' begins. There are many functions of the heart-space, and through different understandings and teachings it is called many things and explained in many ways. But, essentially, it is the place where the gateway to our soul can be found, and where our connection to that which 'Is' can be felt. It is where we feel unconditional love for all things, where we connect to all things, and the place from which healing at every level emanates. It is where we connect to, sense, and discern, *truth* at its deepest level; both the Truth of our soul, and the Truth of that which 'Is'. The heart-space is the cross over point of our 'created-self' and our 'soul-self'; the connection.

This is the place in which we tirelessly strive to live as our true soul-self, and to dissolve our created-self.

The heart-space is the place where we change at a profound level, from *doing*, into *being*. And from 'I' created-self, into 'I am' true soul-self. From love at an intellectual and emotional level, into pure love.

To experience heart-space is an important step on the path towards connection to soul and connection to that which 'Is'; to incarnate and exist as the light and love-filled individual that you truly are.

To help with connecting to and understanding what the heart-space is, it is easier to visualise it, to make it a tangible thing for our minds to begin to grasp. Once our minds focus on this it enables our created-self and spirit-self to connect to our soul. Although our aim is to move above mind-level into heart-level understanding and connection, we need to occupy our mind with something which enables us to focus on our goal, before higher-level connection is made and maintained. A little like giving a baby a rattle, a distraction for mind whilst heart-space is waiting to be felt.

So, if you imagine a ball of pink light, about the size of a large grapefruit, directly below your head, within your chest. Inside this ball of pink light is a small marble-sized ball of white light, this will help when trying to understand what is written. Keep visualising this, and keep *feeling* this space within yourself, as you read this chapter. It will help you sense the truth of what is spoken of. This is how we sense this space as a Passive Receiver.

If you can expand this space so that you are able to sit within it, this is how it feels to exist at heart-space vibration. (If you do this, always return the space to the place and size it came from within you. We are working to raise our consciousness to exist at heart-space/love level of vibration, rather than expand our heart energy centre to sit within heart-space level of vibration).

The heart-space is the space where we experience unconditional love, from that which 'Is' to our soul. It is where we sense the unconditional love from our soul to that which 'Is'. It is where we experience love from our soul to all things, and from all things.

Love, in its purest, most radiant, and most beautiful form.

It is where the blinkers begin to come off our eyes, where we look sideways and begin to realise that we are connected to all things, and that we are part of, and are, all things. This is where we begin to realise that we are a tiny facet of the whole, and that what we say, think, and do, affects everything in existence. If I do to you, I do to myself. If I hurt you, I hurt me, if I love you, I love me.

We begin to sense our connection to everything, and through this connection to all things we begin to feel the love and the pain of all that is around us. It is a profound place of connection, where we begin to feel the unconditional love of that which 'Is', and we begin to understand the profound effect sharing this love with others, and with the planet, can have. This love is not just for humankind, it is for animals, plants, elements, environment, and for all that is. This love expresses itself through our desire to help, to share, to connect, to embrace, to heal and to love all that is. Because all that is, is a part of us, and a part of that which 'Is'.

Through this awareness of heart-space we understand the interconnectedness of all things, of us all being a unique divine aspect of that which 'Is', and our connection to each other as human and spiritual beings. We feel the resonance of unconditional love of all things, and the healing frequency this love brings, both to oneself, but also spilling out into all aspects of that which is around us. We begin to understand our ability to direct this love with *truth* to facilitate healing. It is the place where the healing vibration of love can be channelled from that which 'Is', into the lower-levels of frequency of physical, emotional and mind. This flow of love can be constant and radiating, once we fully inhabit the heart-space way of existence. This constant radiating flow of love frequency will affect everything you encounter, and everywhere you go. Simply by *being*, and existing at this level of vibration, you will be a constant channel for healing, and you will illuminate and ignite those around you, as their heart-space will *hear* the song of the soul and will begin to harmonise with it.

All of this can be felt and experienced within the heart-space frequency. It is the frequency of meditation, contemplation, prayer, love and healing. We can move freely into this space, as we can with all levels of vibrational existence. But the key is to live from this space, exist at this frequency, and occasionally dip into lower frequencies, which we need to do as we are human, and life happens! The essential thing required after we dip out of this level of existence, is to return to this space.

By functioning in our heart-space we can bring together individuals, groups, societies and communities which appear, to all intents and purposes, to be so very different. Through our awareness of our interconnected nature we can identify, celebrate, and connect by acknowledging our core Oneness. With a heart-space overflowing with love, our souls can connect at a level way beyond any difference or comprehension. Our souls resonate in purity and harmony; each one different, and each one totally the same. We will be able to speak to each other at a vibration of truth and harmony. The result of this action communicates way beyond that which is said. The transmission of unconditional love through a word, a look, a gesture, or action, is something which cannot be articulated, only *felt*. As with all things of a higher frequency, or spiritual dimension, they cannot be articulated, only *felt*. And felt not with the five senses, but with our spiritual connection of soul-self. If we can create clarity, awareness, conscious connection to, and incarnation of, our soul, true communication of a divine nature will take place. It is a non-verbal, heart-centred communication of a vibrational, love-filled intent. There will be less need for words, which are empty noises fuelled by misdirected or misinterpreted intent, and there will be more action based on *felt* direction, which will always be guided by love.

When we begin to pull our thoughts/emotions/physical issues into heart-space we begin to sense the relief, or easing of disharmony, within one's being. It may resolve or dissolve the disharmony completely, or it may make one feel easier about the situation. When one finds one's consciousness moving down a vibration into mind or emotion, the pain or disharmony returns. The more we put our mind and emotions into our heart-space, the more loving and harmonious we feel. The emptier our minds, the more we consciously exist in the heart-space, and the easier we feel.

It is imperative this is truly sensed, rather than theorised in the mind. The ease brought about by the returning of consciousness again and again to heart-space, is what causes us to feel more connected to our true nature (soul) and that which 'Is'. It is what begins to motivate us towards the path of heart-space living, and eventually on to soul integration. The more we experience this space/frequency, the more we recognise our true soul-self, our interconnected nature, unconditional love and healing living, and as a result we have a stronger sense of the light of that which 'Is' within the centre of this. Here we can sense our spirit-self's presence, and in time our spirit-self's connection to our soul. As we practice expanding our heart-space and connecting to the real us, our soul, we are preparing our system to exist within this frequency of love, for our soul to incarnate. This is helped even more by the planetary frequencies now existing at heart-space frequency – that of love.

Even if we progress no further than connecting to, and existing as, heart-space, we will share love, heal, sense our interconnectivity, be more receptive to receiving spiritual experience, and ultimately expand and experience our own connection to that which 'Is'.

Once this level of vibration is our conscious way of being, we can work at soul-integration. Once soul-integration has taken place we bring love and light frequency, and permanently experience this level of frequency.

Living as heart-space and living as soul are very different. Heart-space living is first felt by our spirit-self but filtered through the conscious mind. Soul existence just 'is'; living without intent, just *being* love and light. Being your unique divine flame of that which 'Is'.

Heart-space living is living within love and light, soul-self living is living as love and light.

The difference, as with all these things, is difficult to articulate, and can only be lived and felt.

Soul, in the context of heart-space, is our true self. It contains the unique aspect of the divine which was created by that which 'Is' to explore, learn, evolve, and eventually return to, the source of love and light, the source of all that 'Is'. Soul's unique aspect is the incarnate light of that which 'Is', within its very centre, which connects directly to the 'Is' above - the constant emanator of love and light. This is how we can connect to, and develop, our own unique relationship with that which 'Is'. This is the aspect of ourselves which is eternal.

Our soul separates (but stays connected to) a part of itself to create our spirit-self. Soul, via spirit-self, brings its vibration down into the physical to incarnate, but through this incarnation comes the forgetting of itself, through the distraction of living as a human in the physical world.

Our soul enables us to truly understand unconditional love. It is where we understand our interconnected nature and connection to all things. It is where we recognise spiritual experience. It is where we feel, sense, and understand our truth, and the truth of all that is. It is where we feel and receive universal truth and knowledge of all that is, all that was, and all that will be.

It is the thing, which if incarnated into physical self, once our created-self is dissolved and spirit-self reintegrated, will drive the vehicle which is physical, emotional and mind. As we live at present, the physical, emotional and mind created-self tries to drive the soul via the spirit-self. Our spirit-self is between our created-self and our soul. It is affected by the created-self and experiences the potential discomfort this could bring to the soul. It is the buffer between the two. Our spirit-self feels our frustrations, our discordancy, our pain. It tries to communicate between our true-self and our false-self and suffers when one does not hear the other. Therefore, we feel discordant and unfulfilled. We feel lost and lonely, isolated and unloved; because the driver is not driving the car, the directionless car is trying to drive the bound and gagged driver!

So, to begin the process of working towards soul integration the first step we must take is learning to consciously exist within heart-space, rather than visit heart-space.

Consciously existing at heart-space enables the following to be experienced and embodied as a way of living and being:

Love

Heart-space is the frequency of Love.

We experience love from that which 'Is' to our soul.
This is because:

- Soul begins to be felt and connected with at heart-space/love frequency as this is where the gateway to the soul sits.
- There is no coagulated energetic clutter from the lower-levels of vibration of physical, emotional and mind, blocking or clouding the connection.
- The cord of light directly from that which 'Is' above, connects to our own unique aspect of that which 'Is', which sits at the centre of our soul. We can only communicate clearly with our soul, and therefore the light from that which 'Is', when we are within heart-space frequency and above.
- Our own unique aspect of that which 'Is' can receive clear and direct light and love, direct from source, via the clear cord of light from that which 'Is' above. It is felt as light and love

experienced in an over-whelming, indescribable way, which cannot be articulated, only felt as all-consuming, purest, highest-vibrational love and light. We slowly begin to experience this within the vibration of heart-space.

We experience love from our soul-self to that which 'Is'.
This is because:

- We begin to recognise we are a unique facet of that which 'Is', and we are connected to that which 'Is'. This creates a love so deep and profound within oneself, both given and received, that it keeps us tirelessly striving to maintain and develop this connection.
- We recognise at this level of vibration, that much of the low-level discordancy of the physical, emotional and mind is, in fact, irrelevant. This frees us, and brings so much light to us, that it creates profound love because of this new understanding.
- We recognise the love from that which 'Is' to us, and from us to that which 'Is', is the very thing we have been searching for all our lives, in so many ways, and in so many places. The love, understanding, and sense of belonging, has been within us all along. We begin to feel at one when consciously within heart-space.

It is where we experience love for all things and from all things.
This is because:

- At heart-space vibration we become aware of the interconnected nature of all things.
- We recognise we a tiny part of the great Whole.
- We recognise our thoughts and actions effect everything, and everything affects us. There is no *me* – there is only *we*. Therefore, if we wish to receive love, we must give love. We must be love.

- We understand that what I do to you, I do to me. And what I do to me, I do to you. The connection is vibration, and with vibration there are no barriers. We begin to recognise that we are One.

Faith

We connect more strongly with faith in heart-space because:

- Faith is our connection to that which 'Is' above. It can only be sensed. This cord of light is an energetic link which the mind has difficulty rationalising, but the heart senses more strongly. When we sit within heart-space frequency we are in strong and free-flowing connection to soul. Soul has the strong corded link (faith) to that which 'Is' above. Therefore, we have stronger faith when sitting at the frequency of heart-space/love.
- When we are above the frequency of mind and emotions, the conditioning, blocks, coagulations, and ties, which interfere with and block our connection (faith), are less able to influence us. We have clarity of vision and clarity of connection.
- If we can maintain heart-space frequency in our everyday life, rather than popping our consciousness up into it from lower-level vibrations, our faith (connection) becomes stronger, because when it is linked with it strengthens and grows.
- We 'feel' faith rather than 'think' faith.

Trust

It is within the vibration of heart-space that we can begin to truly trust. This is because:

- We have a clear connection to our soul, and our soul has a strong corded connection to that which 'Is' above, therefore we more strongly sense that which 'Is'. The cord of connection is faith. When we sense that which 'Is' through the cord of faith, it enables us to trust. Trust is faith in action.
- When we sit in heart-space, above the mind and emotions, we have far less conflict within ourselves. The mind and emotions have far less influence, enabling trust to grow. When we remove the emotions and mind this creates space; space enables us to *listen*. When we can listen, we sense faith, and trust grows. When trust grows this brings us truth.

Truth

When existing at heart-space we can discern truth. This is because:

- We are not influenced by created-self mind, emotions or physical. We are less influenced by programming, conditioning and circumstance. We sit consciously above these levels, and within the connection to the truth of our soul.
- We are not influenced so much by low-level coagulations of energy, or energetic ties, which also sit within the vibrational levels below heart-space level. They are less able to distort and pull us away from truth.
- We are in free-flowing connection to our soul, with fewer blocks.
   o Our soul is multi-vibrational and sits within the flow of the dynamic, creative that which 'Is'; where the information of that which was, is and will be, exists. It is from this flow that divine truth is received. As soul is not restricted, this flow is received more clearly within spirit-self and passed on to created-self.

- ○ The free-flowing flow of truth is received by the heart, and interpreted in the mind, but is not influenced by, or created by, the mind.
- ○ Free-flowing truth is not influenced by the emotions of our created-self, as within heart-space created-self has little input.
- ○ Within heart-space we can truly begin to sense the difference between mind-knowing and heart-space knowing. Mind-knowing is within the *fact*. Heart-space knowing is within the *Truth*.
- ○ The more truth we sense, and the more we act upon it, the more we recognise that it is always supporting us and leading us the right way. The more we recognise the profound affect working in Truth has on and in our lives, the more we learn to trust, and the more this strengthens our faith.
- Truth enables trust. Trust strengthens faith. Stronger faith enables greater connection to, and flow with, that which 'Is'.

Surrender

When we exist at heart-space we are more easily able to surrender. This is because:

- We do not feel the need to control situations because we have greater trust and faith.
- We are sitting above the mind, emotional, physical frequencies, therefore they are not influencing us. We sit above the conflict these bring.
- We no longer need to control from our ego as we are sitting above ego, within heart-space.
- We are more able to hand our problems/situations into the light for guidance and resolution. This is because we are connected to our soul, which connects us to three things; our

own unique aspect of that which 'Is'; that which 'Is' above; and dynamic, creative, flowing, that which 'Is'. Through surrendering to these three, we have access to all that our unique aspect has within it, all information from dynamic 'Is', and are held in the ultimate love, light and healing of that which 'Is' above. When these three work as one, in surrender, we know all is, and will be, well.

We can now fully surrender, fully at peace.

Stillness

When existing at heart-space we are more able to sit within stillness. This is because:

- We are more able to observe, rather than participate in, thoughts and emotions. We sit above the frequencies of mind and emotions.
- We are no longer pulled and pushed into action by the impulses of our emotions and our programmed thoughts, as we are observing them. We begin to sense whether we need to act upon, or dissolve, that which we are observing.
- We are able to discern in this way because through stillness we enter silence. It is within stillness and silence that we have made space to hear Truth, which can only be heard within the heart.
- Stillness creates a place of balance and centres us. This is because we are not being pulled in any direction and remain within the stillness of centrality to the movement of identity.
- When we are at the centre point of stillness and balance within ourselves, it takes us to the centre of the cord of light, and the centre (or mid) vibrational frequency – heart-space. This is the exact spot to access, and enter through, the gate to our soul-self.

- Imagine a wheel spinning horizontally, its axel being the cord of light. Every possibility of what and who you could be, your thoughts and emotions, are written around the outside of the wheel. You bring your consciousness to the centre of the wheel, pushing none of these things away, and bringing none of them to you. At the centre point there is stillness and silence. None of these things have gone away, but none of them are pulling you out of the centre. You are within the possibility of everything. Then if you imagine the cord of light stretching from the highest vibration – that which 'Is', to the physical body. Imagine half-way up is the mid-vibration; love within heart-space. This is the centre-point vertically. The meeting point of the vertical and the horizontal is where we are aiming for within our energetic system. This is the pin-point gateway and access, through the cord of light, to our soul.
- When we can find ways to sit at the central still point within, we enter through the gateway into the expansive, eternal, peace-filled essence of our soul. In this space we find the stillness within the movement of our soul and hear the wisdom and truth of that which 'Is' loudly within the silence. This experience helps us drop the anchor of deep humility.

Humility

When we exist at heart-space we are more easily able to understand true humility. This is because:

- We more fully connect to that which 'Is', sense our interconnectivity, and open our eyes and heart to the infinite wonder of it all. We understand we are a tiny part of a beautiful whole, and we are in total wonder of this. When we exist at lower-level vibrations we think we are the centre of the universe and everything revolves around us. True humility will not be understood when we exist in this way.

- We value the gifts that heart-space gives us, and shows us, and we realise that possessions and status are not important, and do not define the truth of who we are. We are more able to give up that which we no longer find important, and live a more practically humble life, should we choose to do so. But, as said before, simplicity in existence removes barriers to that which 'Is' but is not an indicator of connection. It can be a tool for connection. True gratitude for what we have and what we are creates humility also, because we are in wonder and true gratefulness for our life, and all that is in it. This is humility in gratitude. Both ways are examples of humility. Both ways, if embraced within heart-space, are ways of walking the path towards the truth of your soul.

When we constantly walk our path considering, embracing, and living, the above qualities, we are slowly but surely dissolving the gateway between our spirit-self and soul-self. We are creating greater connection to our soul-self and that which 'Is'. When we truly live with these qualities in every thought, word and deed, we are living a life in harmony with the truth of our soul. This is when the potential for incarnating and living as soul-self comes to us. Therefore heart-space living is so very important, because this is where the gateway to our true soul-self, and that which 'Is', can be found.

Healing

The constant flow of love and light through us, from that which 'Is' above, is a constant flow of healing. When we exist in heart-space every thought, word, and deed, is of a love/healing vibration. Just by *being* we are radiating love and healing. This love and healing will affect everything we do, everyone we meet, and everywhere we go. When we exist at lower-level vibrations of mind, emotion and physical, our capacity to share love and healing can be clouded by low-level coagulations of energy and created-self thoughts and feelings. It can also be directed by 'mind', whereas healing should be freely guided by heart-space, rather than consciously controlled by created-self. To be a clear channel for healing we need to occupy heart-space more fully. To facilitate healing more efficiently we need to heal ourselves first, to be a clear channel and a conduit for bringing love and healing to all. Through our awareness of our interconnectivity, and being an efficient channel for healing and love, we can play our part in the change the planet and humanity needs.

Dissolving Energy

Dissolving of the three lower levels of vibration can take place more easily when we consciously sit within the level of heart-space vibration. This is because:

- We are at the vibration of healing. When we pull thoughts, emotions and issues into the vibration of heart-space they are resolved more easily and healed more easily.
- We are not so influenced by our minds, emotions and programming. We can attend to the issues at hand more dispassionately, so they can be resolved more rationally.
- When we are in the vibration of Truth, we *know* what is right to do, even if we do not understand why. We are more able to *listen*.
- We are more able to surrender and allow that which 'Is' to guide our healing/dissolving.
- When a coagulation of energy is dissolved it creates space/fluidity. When sitting within heart-space vibration, that space is filled with love. The more love flows within the energetic system, the more we can be, and share, love and healing. This growing of heart-space vibration, and creation

of fluidity within our energetic field, creates the right environment for soul-self to potentially fully incarnate.

Spiritual experience

We are more receptive to spiritual experience because:

- We are more able to sense *Truth*, and decipher the difference between mental projection, spiritual experience, and experience of that which 'Is'.
- We can consciously connect to higher vibrations where we are more able to access spiritual experience, because we are above the vibrations of mind, emotions and physical. We are not influenced by the mind, emotions or physical, and we are not blocked by coagulations at these levels. Our access and connections are clearer, as our consciousness can flow more freely up our cord of connection to the levels of spiritual connection.
- We are more connected to our soul, therefore spiritual experience and information is passed to us from soul via spirit-self, directly to our consciousness, because we are at a more receptive level of vibration.
- The dynamic, creative, free-flowing information from that which 'Is' moves freely within soul, therefore when we sit within heart-space, where we connect to our soul, we are in clearer, receptive flow of that information.
- We more strongly connect to all, as this is where we sense our interconnectivity, and are therefore more sensitive to that which is around us.
- We are within the flow of healing/love which connects us to all, as we flow with it, and connect through it.
- The heart-space is the space of contemplation and listening, and when we are in contemplation and listening, we are more able to receive spiritual guidance.

When we are within lower-levels of vibration there may be distractions and blocks to the flow of information, and we do not listen. In lower-levels we are more likely to respond mentally or emotionally and try to influence or categorise that which we receive, rather than just *being* with the information/experience. Passive Receivers need to be in a receptive space in order to receive clearly.

- When we have spiritual experience, whilst existing at heart-space, we do not define ourselves by it (ego), which tethers it, and us, to low-level vibration, therefore pulling us out of heart-space vibration. We also sit within the flow, therefore spiritual experience comes and goes, and we trust it will come again. There is no need to hang on to it, and less likelihood that what should be a transient gift will later become a blockage.

So, if we can sit within the heart-space frequency of love and healing, we are more able to resolve and heal energetic issues within ourselves. We are more able to sense and work with our interconnectivity. We are more able to connect to that which 'Is' and connect with our soul. Our faith will strengthen, our trust will increase, our sense of truth will heighten, and our capacity to surrender will become easier. We will be more able to decipher mind experience, spiritual experience and 'Is' experience. We will radiate love, light, and healing, in all that we say, think and do, which will begin to reach and affect all. We lead by example rather than dictate. We become the change we wish to see in the world. We light the heart-space of others. We will live in, and with, divine 'Truth'. We will live as *we* rather than *me*. We begin to create the energetic environment which will allow the soul to incarnate in this lifetime.

This is when the real changes in ourselves, and in the world, begin.
Everything begins with heart-space.
Everything begins with love...

Connection

We are all connected – at every level.

In the physical we are all vibrations; energy that vibrates at a lower frequency into physical form.

Sound frequencies, light frequencies, thought frequencies.

All vibrating at the same time, all creating a cacophony at the same time.

An orchestra of vibrations; each one seemingly independent, but each affecting the other.

Each connected to the other – nothing in isolation.

So, each thought, word, and deed, rippling out to integrate and resonate with the 'whole'.

No matter how isolated we feel, we are connected and part of the 'all'.

Therefore, we cannot fight against this connection, as this causes conflict and disharmony.

If we pull back, or pull away from our connection, we are creating blockages and stagnation.

We need fluidity, movement, 'being'.

If we freely 'be' part of 'all' we are light, connected, free-flowing, fresh and 'breathing' in a spiritual way.

Harmony.

Harmony is all things vibrating together to create something beautiful,

IS-BEING

something far greater than the sum of its parts.

This separation from all, this disharmony, is created
by mind.
Mind tries to categorise, separate, understand and
'know'.
It needs to master and control.
It is a survival mechanism.
But trying to bring control to an interconnected whole
is an impossible task.
We will fail, and with this failure comes ego, therefore
ego tries harder, and the spiral loops
downwards.
If we do not categorise, give rank to, and separate all
that is, we give it freedom.
Freedom to 'be'.
Freedom to reach its true potential and beyond.

If we label and rank things, we take away their
potential, their potency, their ability to be
different, to do different, to make changes in
unimaginable ways.
There is infinite potential.
We need to understand everyone has infinite
potential if we give them the freedom to 'be';
if there is freedom of thought and of
connection.
If we can encourage humans to connect to 'Truth'
through heart-space and allow for infinite

165

potential to realise creative thinking and doing, then new ways, new understanding and new humanity can arise.

This cannot be done with restrictions of societal 'norms', hierarchy, segregation, conditioning and control.

There needs to be more freedom to 'be', to bring higher spiritual vibration through acceptance of the new.

But the crux is that this must be through the heart-space and not the 'mind'.

Through heart-space it is for the greater good of all, for peace, harmony and balance; for beauty, connection and love.

If we bring freedom and disseminate it via 'mind' we loop back into segregation, hierarchy, control and ego.

And this, in turn, blocks flow, growth and raising of vibration.

The thing required is heart-space connection. When we are truly functioning from this space alone there is no blockage to potential.

Potential for all that is, to be free, to be brought into this world.

To create a world in truth, beauty, harmony and love.

Heart-space is key...

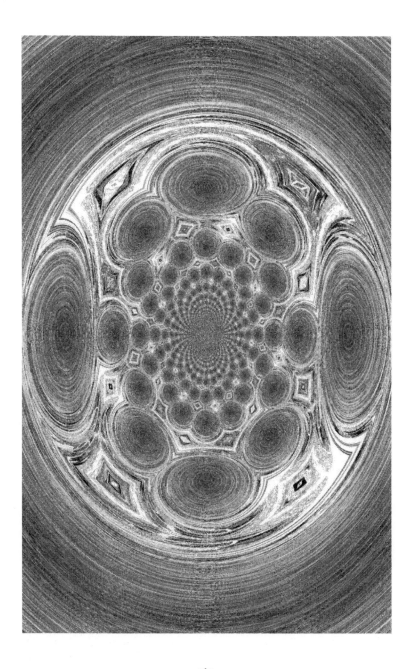

Mel Cross

SPIRITUAL EXPERIENCE

Experiential signposts

Spiritual experiences are thoughts, sensations, visions etc. which are beyond physical explanation. There are many things that we experience as human beings which can appear unusual, strange, or beyond that which is usually experienced. Perhaps they are ordinary thoughts, dreams, or day-dreams, or brought about through drugs, physical or mental illness, or stress. But sometimes these experiences cannot be explained in these ways.

The mind is an incredibly complex system and can produce an enormous range of experiences. But spiritual experience produces a very different *feeling* as, energetically, it is produced from a much higher frequency of vibration. Those who can sense the difference of vibration are more able to flag up when a thought is produced from a spiritual vibration, rather than from the vibration of the meandering mind. It has a very different feeling, and a very defined clarity to it. Almost like the mind is an old black and white television, and spiritual experience is more of an ultra HD television picture.

When your experience or thought is produced by spirit, once you can sense the difference, you will really notice it. This spiritual experience/thought is fed into the conscious mind from soul-self, via spirit-self, to mind. Or it can be passed from spirit or guides, via spirit-self, to mind.

What are guides and what is their role?

Many people talk of their experiences of guides and working with guides. Guides work via different levels of spiritual vibration to pass information or confirmation to us. They interpret that which we need to understand from information from 'grid' (dynamic, creative 'Is'), spirit, or information from our soul.

As Passive Receivers, we do not yet have the capacity to freely and consistently receive soul information, or grid information, therefore guides work as translators for us. They can appear in our mind's eye in many forms, but usually recognisably human in character. Many people build up very intimate relationships with their guides and trust them implicitly to guide and support them as they walk their spiritual path.

The guides which translate information from one's own soul are often projections of previous incarnations of one's soul or are emotionally accessible manifestations of form to the individual. Guides which interpret information from 'grid' or spiritual dimensions, are spirit and independent to one's soul. Sometimes people known to the individual, who have passed over, will assist one on one's journey, as do beings of the angelic realms.

The trust which is built up between an individual and their guides is of utmost importance, for the reassurance of the *truth* of the spiritual/Is understanding that comes to them. Then later, when they begin to work within heart-space and connect to their own soul, they need to *trust* implicitly the sensation of *truth* within themselves. This trust and sense of truth will be recognised by the same feeling of peace and certainty which is experienced when receiving information via the comforting, supporting presence of guides.

Spiritual experiences may take the form of conversations with guides, visions, vivid dreams or meaningful co-incidences, for example.

All this interaction is for us to begin to connect to, and then interpret, these sensations and images. This helps us grow our ability to *listen* and deepens our sensitivity to more subtle information. These experiences are for us to be able to learn to discern that which is produced *by* the 'mind' and that which is produced from *beyond* the mind.

Once people begin to have spiritual experiences, they may seek more and more of these. This is when people begin trying to consciously connect to information, perhaps through meditation, interaction with guides, dowsing and so on. But one must be careful if one does not have a good teacher to help support you in this work. There are many basics to be learned, and many pitfalls of such work, if you do not have the tools and understanding to work safely. Spiritual experience can be so incredibly beautiful that individuals want to access it all the time, but this must be done with care. Not all spiritual experiences are positive. Not all those purporting to be guides are positive. Malevolence can interfere with even the most experienced spiritual workers. Guidance, support and safety when working is required so as not to cause oneself great harm.

Why do we need to work with spiritual experience and with our guides?

Spiritual experience is incredible for many reasons. But spiritual experience has one main important purpose, which is sometimes lost completely by some energy/spiritual workers.

Spiritual experience is a signpost directing us towards ascending the connection to our own soul, and our own unique aspect of that which 'Is'. Spiritual experience is for each of us to be guided on our path towards heart-space living and full soul-integration.

Each experience gives us tools for the journey and signposts to the path.

Spiritual experience is a side-effect of the path of spiritual evolution, it is not the goal of spiritual evolution.

Spiritual experience is a signpost towards that which 'Is' experience – which is what one begins to experience when working on heart-space living and soul-integration. 'Is' experience is beyond description and is ultimate love, ultimate peace, ultimate light. It is very different from spiritual experience as it comes from 'Is' above (ultimate peace, light and love) rather than from spirit. When one understands and experiences 'Is', one understands the importance of the path of ascending towards oneself and that which 'Is', rather than becoming distracted by the scattering of spiritual experiences.

Once soul integration has taken place, spiritual experience changes. It is flowing rather than sought. It is lived, rather than given to us. The guidance one feels within oneself, and which is given to give to others, just 'Is'.

It is flowing truth, rather than given truth.

Pitfalls of spiritual experience

Spiritual experiences can be incredible things, both positively and negatively. They show us the possibilities of what is 'beyond' our physical comprehension, and a taste of the potential capabilities of us as spiritual/soul beings. They are a means of helping us understand and read the signposts directing us on our spiritual journey, and they help teach us. They help us connect to our guides or those in spiritual realms who wish to help us. They give us tools to deal with energetic connection and give us a greater understanding of that which 'Is'. Ultimately, they grow our trust; In our own sensitivity, our own interpretation, our own understanding, and our trust in that which 'Is'. But, as this trust begins to grow, and we begin to learn to differentiate *truth*, this is where we can become unstuck.

The beauty, joy, understanding and vibration of spiritual experience can become addictive and eventually become contorted into something quite different. Often an individual, although beginning with good intention, can unknowingly be guided along an altogether different path. Although all experiences are learning experiences, and all paths lead you the right way eventually, it is up to us to take responsibility for where we travel, and how we travel. We have been blessed with many gifts, and it is up to us to honour these gifts and treat them with the respect and love with which they were revealed to us.

So, what are the pitfalls of the journey? Firstly, we may take 'ownership' of the gift. We have a certain amount of gift, we claim it, protect it, and keep it to the exclusion of all things. 'I have the gift of healing' for example. 'It is mine, I own it, my way is the right way.' We keep it to ourselves, we do not share it, and it makes us feel we 'have' something, rather than bumbling along ordinarily in everyday life. By owning it, we begin to label ourselves with this spiritual gift. 'I am a healer'. By using the gift as a definition, a label, a way to assert some form of 'one-upmanship', we create an energetic tether to the gift we possess. The gift in and of itself is a gift of higher-level vibration. So, as a healer, we understand healing comes from the heart-space level of vibration. If we acknowledge the gift of healing at the heart-space level of vibration, love it, work with it, wonder at it, be humble with it, and trust it, it will stay a gift of heart-space vibration. If we do these things, but do not tie it to our identity, it stays at heart-space. If we acknowledge, but let go of the definition, let it free, let it breathe, let it grow and let it be what it is, it will stay a gift and stay at heart-space vibration. When we let it go, we enable it to continue growing and evolving, we let it flow with and through us, rather than holding on to it. This keeps it fluid, flowing, alive and 'Is' filled.

The problem is, when we are still functioning from our physical, emotional, mind vibration, we tend to cling on to the gift. We hold it, own it, and define ourselves by it. Those actions tether energetic cords to the gift or spiritual experience. These tethers, because they are formed by our emotions or mind, hold the gift or the experience anchored at low-level vibration. These cords are created because we are still functioning from our mind/created-self (ego). We feel we need the security that defining our experiences and gifts brings. We feel superior to others because of that which we experience or do. We use these experiences to rank ourselves against other energy or spiritual workers. We begin to feel insecure about what we do, and what others do, in a spiritual capacity. We keep our knowledge to ourselves and decry other people's knowledge, gifts and experiences. All of this is to create a ranking or hierarchy of energy/spiritual workers. All these thoughts and actions tether us to low-level vibration, no matter how gifted we are, or what experiences we have had. Some of us are exceptionally gifted energy/spiritual workers, but if our ego and created-self are not working with us, to help us on our path to dissolving our lower levels of vibration, our true-soul potential will only be glimpsed, but not incarnated; worked with, but not maintained. Our gifts and experiences can be nurtured, grown and expanded, but whilst they are tethered by ego, they anchor us in low-level vibrational existence, therefore heart-space living, and true soul-integration will not fully take place.

There are so many energy/spiritual workers, and people of faith, who earnestly believe they are walking the path, but they are blinded to the fact they are walking it tethered to the physical, emotional and mind. Only when all experiences and gifts are acknowledged, thanked, understood, embraced and then let go of, will the raising of vibration truly begin to take place in an individual. The crux comes because when we work from these lower levels we are constrained in ego, and to move beyond ego into humility, to acknowledge where we truly are, takes bravery, love, faith, trust and surrender, where we enter stillness, to truly sense truth.

The very action of letting go of spiritual experience/gift/identity, is the very thing that brings it closer to us. When we let go, this brings us more spiritual experience and connection. When we don't hold on, it comes closer to us, as we raise our vibration and become more connected and more able to exist within spiritual experience. When we hold on to it, we lower its vibration into emotion and mind and negate or slow down the opportunity for growth and expansion.

We must let go of the very thing that we seek,
so that we may truly find it.

Spiritual experience can distract us greatly from our path, if our path is to connect to heart-space, and ultimately incarnate our soul-self in this lifetime. Spiritual experience can turn our eyes away from our path completely. But this is as it should be. If you are distracted by the glittering, mesmerising treasures of spiritual experience, then perhaps you need to work on the qualities required to make true connection to that which 'Is'. Distraction alerts us to what is required.

If you are solely working in love, faith, trust, truth, surrender, stillness and humility, then you are less likely to turn towards spiritual experience, and more likely to keep total focus on 'Is' connection. The signposts of spiritual experience are there to point us onto the path towards our true potential, and to give us the skills and experiences required to step forwards along this path. If spiritual experiences are a distraction to you, then they ensure your destination will not be reached unless you return to walking in humility, and with purity of intent. The things that point you towards your path are the same things that lure you away from it. That choice is yours, as with all things.

If your path is to work with your incredible energetic and spiritual gifts, and not walk the path towards full soul-integration, then this is also good, if the gifts are used with one eye focused on the light of that which 'Is'. All things happen when they are right, and each and everybody's path is right for them, whatever they choose it to be.

If you are an energy or spiritual worker, whether you choose to walk the path to soul-integration or not, please use your incredible gifts and insight to gently guide, nurture, and support those who come to you. Please help them to find their feet and manage their path. This is a most blessed gift indeed; to help provide part of the map for those that journey. Support, not push, facilitate, not lecture, and encourage self-growth, rather than creating them to become reliant on you. Those who journey need the tools to journey alone, whilst holding the hand of that which 'Is'. Help them to trust and to find their way to their own truth.

And finally, thank you for being beautiful you – and all the tireless work you do for the good of all.

WORKING WITH OUR ENERGY SYSTEM

Transforming and

evolving

s we prepare ourselves for the transformation from our spirit-self Passive Receiver, to soul-self Dynamic Creator, we need to be aware of, take care of, and address, the requirements and effects of our evolving and changing energetic system.

The energy system, as it stands as a Passive Receiver, is a system of single layers of energetic vibration. The densest layer closest to our physical body, the finest layer on the outer edges of our energy system. In simplistic terms, the layers are as follows:

- Physical
- Emotional
- Mental
- Heart-space

- Communication
- Spiritual
- 'Is' connection

The physical layer being closest to our physical body, and other layers radiating out from there. These layers hold information and coagulations from our experiences in this lifetime, and occasionally coagulations which need addressing from other lifetimes.

These layers are fluid and fluctuating, but still operate separately, as they are of different vibrations. Once we are existing, or working to exist at heart-space vibration, we need to work on our energetic system so that it is clear enough to progress on to soul-self integration.

The three layers which need to be constantly worked upon are the physical, emotional, and mind layers. These layers are the ones constructed by soul to incarnate spirit-self in this lifetime. For soul to be able to fully integrate in this lifetime these layers need to be clear. This is for two reasons.

The first reason is that for soul to be able to integrate, the energetic system needs to be as pure as it can be; stripped back to that which it was when it was born; returning to the original 'pattern'. This is because we need to be harmonious in our thought, word and deed, in every moment, so that we cause no disharmony to our soul-self. If our energy system is clear it means there are no coagulations holding us stiff, distorted and cluttered. Our system will be clear and free-flowing. This free-flowing movement creates space for multi-vibrational soul-self to begin to integrate as the layers are less defined and less separated.

The second reason is that the removal of coagulated energy in the three lower levels means there is less holding us and our conscious gaze at the vibrations of physical, emotion and mind. This means we are more able to move and exist within heart-space vibration. There is less holding us and tethering us down at lower levels, and it is easier for us to raise into heart-space vibration. The more we can stay in heart-space vibration, the more we sense, the more we sense, the more easily we can clear. When we do this, we can see and feel the benefits of being at this vibration and clearing coagulations, so we work more eagerly on this.

When we work to clear coagulations of energy (experiences/emotions/patterning disharmonious to our soul/that which 'Is') it is important we work at this from four angles.

We must address and work on our:

1. Physical – Changing our circumstances or surroundings, addressing our physical requirements or health.
2. Emotions – Retraining our emotional responses to things and undoing emotional patterns from the experience of living in this lifetime. Using our emotional responses as signposts to that which needs to be addressed. If you have a disproportionate emotional reaction to a thought, situation or circumstance it is usually indicative of something which needs addressing at a physical/emotional/mind/energetic level.
3. Mind – Rewiring and amending our thoughts, behaviours, programming, in a way conducive to heart-space living and harmonious to our soul.
4. Energetic – As we become more energetically sensitive, we can sense more easily the blockages and coagulations which need to be addressed/removed in a practical energetic way. This removal can be instant and undertaken by that which 'Is', but we are, as a true soul-self divine aspect of that which 'Is', able to take responsibility for, and work with, our own energetic systems.

This is where we begin to transform from Passive Receiver (inert acceptance/non-awareness of energetic issues) to Dynamic Creator (active and consistent carer of, and attender to, energetic issues.)

The origins of coagulation

Coagulation of energy is where an experience, which created disturbance or disharmony to one's soul-self created a blockage, distortion or lump of discordant energy. This can then be held in a layer of energetic vibration within one's energy field. This discordant lump of energy will stay until it is dissolved or harmonised in some way. This may be through positive thought, positive action, energy clearing, or dissolved by that which 'Is'.

The coagulation will draw attention to itself by creating an emotion/thought when you are experiencing something similar, in order for you to address the coagulation. But often, when emotion arises that signposts a need for action, we as human beings and Passive Receivers, do that which soothes our painful emotion. I.e.; we tend to run away from, redirect, or blame someone or something else for our distress and disharmony. When we do not address our disharmony, it allows the disharmonious energy to be built upon, layer after layer, which allows the coagulation to grow. For example, if someone says or does something mean to us it may cause us distress and disharmony. In the future we may choose to run away from situations or people similar to those involved. We may avoid situations. We may blame people. We may label similar people the same way. We may react defensively or aggressively in similar situations. We may create pre-emptive arguments to avoid similar circumstance. We may label ourselves and believe what was said, and then build our personality, reactions and perspectives or perceptions on that single word or situation which created the discordant coagulation.

One small incident can cause a lifetime of disharmony due to the coagulation which was created. Emotional reaction signposts this disharmony. We may need to work mentally, emotionally, and/or energetically to remove this disharmony. When we do not address the root causes of disharmony, we very often create larger disharmony, because our subsequent reactions and actions are also disharmonious to our soul. We then behave, because we have not addressed issues, in a way which causes great pain and distress to ourselves. We create our own misery, our own disharmony, and our own discordant coagulations.

Energy identification and addressing takes a brave person. We must look deep into that which we most try to avoid.

Coagulation Identification

If we are going to begin clearing our discordant energy from our three lower levels of vibration, we first need to be able to identify these coagulations.

There are various ways of doing this.

The role of pain

Pain draws our attention to that which needs to be addressed. Whether it be energetic, spiritual, mental, emotional or physical. Pain in all its guises draws attention to issues and, through the discomfort it causes, forces us to act. If we do not act to relieve pain, the pain and the cause of the pain grows. Therefore, the coagulated energy will grow from the discordant nature of the pain. This cycle of pain needs to be ended and harmonised.

There are two main stimulators of action and change – one is love, and the other is pain.

Pain causes us to act, it causes us to take note and it flags things up. Removal of pain is a very basic animal instinct. It is what stimulates our survival mechanism. Physical pain is for our physical survival. Emotional pain is learned.

If we are laying in the sun and get overheated, this causes us physical pain, this causes distress (emotion), which makes us move into the shade. Thus, keeping us safe. If we did not have the physical pain, we would not move. If the physical pain did not cause the pain of distress emotionally, we would not move. Physical pain helps us to protect ourselves physically.

If someone hurts our feelings, we are bullied, or we suffer a loss, for example, these are things which may cause us emotional pain. This stimulates us to find ways of negating us experiencing the pain again. We alter our behaviour, we find ways of dealing with, moving from, or removing the causes of emotional pain from ourselves. Emotional pain makes us find ways to protect ourselves emotionally. These actions are learned. Pain, in its various ways, causes us to move, change and try to relieve the painful situation. We would do anything to remove ourselves from the pain, or do anything to remove the pain from ourselves, both for physical and emotional pain.

When we are working with our energetic system and are trying to create fluidity in our three lower levels of vibration, we often must behave in a manner opposite to the way we have been genetically, mentally or emotionally programmed. To heal pain, we must walk towards it. We must recognise it, walk towards it, grasp it, examine it, and work with it mentally, emotionally and energetically. Then we must embrace, dissolve and accept it with open arms. To walk towards our soul, and our connection to that which 'Is', we walk towards pain.

And we walk in pain.

Pain helps us learn, helps us grow, helps us understand and enables our faith in that which 'Is' to become stronger, as that which 'Is' helps us understand, deal with, resolve and heal that which causes us distress. Pain helps us create a stronger relationship with that which 'Is'. We walk towards pain to dissolve, clear and heal it. We also walk in it, because once we have experienced the brief touch of that which 'Is', we spend the rest of our lives in pain, desperately trying to reconnect to that experience of love. It is the pain of separation which keeps us walking on and on, no matter how tough it gets. This is so we can eventually live in the bliss, peace, love and harmony of our permanent conscious connection to that which 'Is'.

If we consciously work at identifying and removing coagulations of energy because of our pure love for that which 'Is', our love for the divine facet of that which 'Is' inside us, and because we want to share love with all by being the best that we can be, this is the most incredible way to work. We work motivated by love, in all its guises, rather than working motivated by pain.

Recognition of reactions

Often our disharmonious coagulated energy is buried so deep in our psyche that it is difficult to know it is there, let alone recognise it and act upon it. Pain is one way to recognise it, whether it be physical, emotional, mental, spiritual or energetic. Another way is to take more notice of oneself and one's reactions to situations and circumstances. When we have an emotional or behavioural reaction to something, which on reflection, is slightly disproportionate or incompatible with the circumstances which provoked it, it is probably worth exploring. It can be an indicator of something which needs resolution and dissolving within oneself. When this happens, we need to take a breath, step outside oneself and into heart-space, and view what has happened from the outside – like a dispassionate observer. Look at the trigger, look at the reaction. What has caused the reaction/distress and how did you respond? Can you work to respond differently? Can you change the trigger or situation? What can you do differently? How can you think differently? How can you behave differently?

When we begin to look at ourselves and address things and change, to bring more peace/balance/harmony and a proportional response to things, coagulations of energy may begin to dissolve. If we are viewing from the heart-space, we are viewing from the healing vibration. But we must remember our thoughts, emotions, behaviours and reactions need to *truly* change, deep within us. To play at change, rather than truly changing, means things will rarely resolve or dissolve. The created-self is very good at convincing itself that it is changing – but spirit-self/soul-self will know different. In fact, it can cause further distress because the tension created between created-self and spirit-self will actually cause disharmony.

You can never fool your soul!

Authenticity in all things is required for true soul-evolution.

When we have an emotional reaction which affects us, this is a wonderful indicator of work to be done, and we should be thankful for this.

An emotional/mind-based reaction to a situation or circumstance is also indicative that one is still operating from the emotional/mind levels of vibration. It shows we are not operating from within our heart-space. This is also a 'flag'. If we are existing at the level of heart-space vibration and an emotional/challenging situation arises, we dip into emotional/mind level of vibration – and this is right. We are still human after all. But if we do not reasonably quickly return to a state of peaceful mind within heart-space, we are still not operating from heart-space frequency. If we are in heart-space frequency we return to it within a day or so, and from there we can peacefully and mindfully deal with the issue at every level; practically, physically, emotionally, mentally and energetically. We will be in a vibration of healing and connection to truth (our soul-self) and this will help us dispassionately deal with all things at all levels. It will facilitate harmonising and dissolving any coagulated discordant energy and begin the multi-level healing process.

Therefore, pain or emotional response helps us gauge how far we have evolved and what work we will still have to do.

If we have worked at addressing our three lower levels of coagulated energy from a position of heart-space, everything will be easier for us. We can more easily recognise when something is discordant with our soul as we are in the vibration which connects to our soul – the link between spirit-self and soul-self. This strong connection is more sensitive to disharmony. The signpost will be bigger, stronger and more greatly felt. This is because soul does not contain physical, emotional and mind vibration, so coagulations/disharmony in these layers of spirit-self are flagged up strongly when consciously connected to soul.

If we are operating from heart-space frequency our energetic system is clearer, which means disharmony is sensed more easily as it stands out more.

If we operate at heart-space vibration, we are within the healing vibration of that which 'Is'. Everything is in a constant flow of healing and everything is dealt with more easily. Even by consciously sitting at this frequency, healing is constantly flowing just by *being*, and the possibility of coagulation clearance, even without conscious effort, can take place. This is because when existing at heart-space frequency we are connecting to our soul, and our soul has a greater and stronger connection to that which 'Is', the emanator of healing.

Also, by being in heart-space frequency we are more aware of our connection to all things and each other. This awareness and increased sensitivity to connection also help us to be more aware of how we respond to others and how others respond to us. This awareness of connection helps us flag up more easily unhealthy dynamics, unneeded cords or tethers of energy to others, and our reactions to and from others. These reactions usually help us flag up, and point to, disharmonious coagulation.

Clearing coagulations; and cords, hooks and ties

There are many ways to begin to address coagulations of stuck/stagnant/discordant energy within the physical, emotional and mind levels of vibration within one's energetic system.

The first thing to do is to identify a coagulation. This can be brought about by the sign-posts of pain or emotional/mental disharmony. But, if we become more aware of, and attuned to, our own energetic system, we can begin to address things from two angles. If we sense disharmony, we can address our physical/emotional/mental situation. This will begin to harmonise us at a human level, which will help energetic issues to resolve. Or, we can identify discordant/coagulated energy in our energetic systems and work to harmonise our energy. This will help us address the causes of the disharmony as the blockage which was holding us in an unmovable physical/emotional/mental place will be removed, thus allowing freedom of flow, freedom of situation, and freedom for healing to take place.

If we can check, identify, harmonise and heal our own energetic systems, we will journey more efficiently and more fluidly towards heart-space living, and on to soul-integration. Taking responsibility for our energetic system is key to spiritual progression. We keep our bodies healthy, we keep our emotions healthy and we keep our minds healthy. We need to keep our energetic systems healthy too.

There are many methods for identifying and clearing energetic coagulations, which I won't go in to in this book. This text is purely to help raise your awareness of energy work, and its potential to help you on your path towards that which 'Is'. This is a 'basic' overview, rather than an 'in-depth' view, and will be expanded upon, I am sure, in another text. There is an abundance of energy-workers out there, so go and find guidance. If you do find someone to help you, trust your instincts and your sense of truth. If something doesn't feel quite right - it isn't right!

To be able to identify and clear energetic coagulations you will need to find a wise and trusted teacher to guide you as you begin to work with yourself. In this instance, energy work is about developing and working on 'self' to raise awareness, increase sensitivity and to progress. It is not about searching out people to work *on* you. It is about learning how *you* can work on you. This is very important!

Your greatest teacher of energy work – is you! You just have to learn to listen, trust your 'guides', and begin to sense 'Truth'. After that, you will be guided.

As well as coagulations of energy, there are also energetic cords and tethers. These are energetic links made and maintained, between you and other people, and you and situations. These people, on occasion, may even be those who have passed over, or who are from other lifetimes. These energetic links are made and dissolved as we connect to people and disconnect from people, sometimes fleetingly, sometimes for a whole lifetime. It is like setting up an energetic bond or communication line between you and another. Sometimes these links are healthy, for example between two friends who love each other and treat each other with consideration, kindness and respect. This is a two-way healthy cord/connection; energy moves both ways and freely. Or you can have more unhealthy connections, which is where the relationship is unbalanced, or not conducive to healthy relationships and growth. For instance, a needy connection can be made from a mother to a child. The mother demands attention and feeds energetically, through the energetic cord, upon the energy of the ever-guilty child. In every encounter, and even when apart (energy cords stretch any distance and through many lifetimes) the energetic feeding will take place. Energy will be drained from the child and absorbed by the mother. This draining cord may, for example, create guilt, resentment, fear, anger or resigned surrender from the child as it can find no way to end the cycle/pattern of energy drain. The mother will always rely on the energy being brought to her via the energetic cord, to maintain her demanding and needy requirements. Whilst this energetic dynamic remains, both parties are held in their subsequent positions of master and victim. Neither party may even be aware of these exchanges, as they may have been set up through circumstance and have been unknowingly maintained. It is very often difficult for either party to change this situation. As I have said before, it takes behavioural/mind changes and emotional awareness to attend to effects on our physical human selves. And, even more beneficially, it takes the energetic awareness of the individuals to address the dynamics of the energetic cording. If both approaches are attended to, the benefits are monumental.

Also, there are energetic hooks and ties which are established in much the same manner – through situations and circumstances, but function slightly differently. They are very often not an exchange mechanism for energetic movement and communication, but are binds which tether you to certain people, events or situations. They hold you in place when really things need to be detached for you to move on, change and grow. This detaching is found within the act of forgiveness.

The cords, hooks and ties can be simple or complex and can make such a monumental difference to your spiritual/soul development once removed, dissolved, addressed or balanced. Often these issues are best dealt with, but be aware that sometimes they have been set up to keep you in a healthy place, or are beneficial to you at this moment. Sometimes there is a right time for work to be done, but it isn't always when you *think* it should be! They may also serve as a learning opportunity or an opportunity for growth. Listen to your sense of *Truth*, it will guide you as to what is right, and when or if it is the right time for action.

The benefits of working on cords, hooks and ties are huge for your journey towards heart-space living and soul integration. Once removed and/or harmonised, this creates freedom of energetic movement between layers and can rebalance your energy field, changing the dynamics of situations and relationships which hold you in place. And, once addressed, can help you raise your vibration to heart-space frequency rather than, quite literally, holding you in place within the lower levels of vibration.

Again, you need a wise and experienced teacher, and you need to listen to your own truth and develop your own energetic sensitivity and understanding. EVERYONE can do this if they work on it. But, something also to bear in mind, is that if you are very uncomfortable about working on yourself in an energetic way, you can use prayer or conscious direction to incredible effect.

Prayer, in this instance, is the conscious direction of intent towards an issue for its resolution. Therefore, if you sense an energetic issue you can place it in the hands of that which 'Is' for it to be resolved. Participation in prayer consciously directs your intent, and the energetic connection of the soul-self, towards resolution of an issue. It also serves to remind you of your constant connection to that that which 'Is', and that that which 'Is' is always flowing within you, and working with you, to bring resolution and harmonisation. Energy work and prayer serve a similar purpose. Prayer brings conscious awareness and connection to that which 'Is', to bring about change, resolution, and harmonisation. But with energy work we become active participants in our growth and evolution, rather than a passive observer of our growth and evolution. That which 'Is' is always working with us, within us and through us, whichever way we choose to move forwards, either with prayer or energy work, as long as we always work with purity of intent and within light and love.

Removal of energetic coagulation, cords and ties is essential for heart-space living and for walking your path towards integration of true soul-self. And, as I have said before, this can be done through working at a physical/practical level, an emotional level and a mind level as these can bring about energetic changes. But if we can consciously work at physical/emotional/mind *and* energetically, we will progress so much more efficiently, smoothly and more quickly than when only working on our minds, emotions and physical circumstance. The constant attending to, and removal of, energetic coagulations in the energetic field, and the attending to, and removal of, cords and ties which do not serve us positively, will help enable the following to happen.

Free-flowing movement within our energy system

Free-flowing movement within our energy system is essential for evolving from spirit-self into soul-self. The freedom of movement within the energy system allows more freedom of movement of consciousness between the layers of vibration. This movement, once the energy system begins to be cleared, allows more fluidity and flow. The fluidity and flow begin to acclimatise one's system to the free-flowing movement of multi-vibrational existence of soul. Soul requires a free-flowing unrestricted energetic field in order to integrate. Any blockages or discordancy which holds one in lower-level vibration hinders soul-self integration. For multi-vibrational soul-self to incarnate one needs to clear the three lower-levels of one's energy system. Soul cannot sit within the vibrations of physical, emotional and mind, as these vibrational levels do not exist at soul-self level. Soul-self exists at heart-space vibration and above. When we incarnate as spirit-self we split into single layered vibrational existence and create the physical, emotional and mind layers. So, to integrate soul in this lifetime these three layers need to be clear and free-flowing, otherwise soul cannot integrate comfortably.

As the planetary vibration has raised into heart-space vibration to accommodate soul evolution, it is only now that our soul has the perfect environment in which to integrate. Whilst the planet stayed at physical, emotional, mind vibration it was much more difficult for soul to integrate, and for enlightened existence to follow on behind this. This will now all change due to the planetary vibrational shift, and our new understanding.

When we begin to clear our lower three levels of existence it is like taking off a tight corset. It allows deeper breath, greater movement and more connection to all layers of vibration. It creates space, harmony and the environment to support and protect the newly inhabited soul.

When there is clearance of the three lower levels of vibration of coagulations of energy, and there is free-flowing movement of energy and conscious awareness, AND one begins to consciously exist at the heart-space frequency, this is the perfect environment for soul-self integration. Existence at the vibration of heart-space/love, and no pulling down into lower frequencies due to total clearance of lower frequencies, creates the perfect environment to begin the process of soul integration. Soul cannot integrate into a restricted or blocked energetic system. Because it is multi-vibrational it requires a fluid energetic system to be multi-vibrational. Constrictions or blocks at lower levels of vibration stifle fluidity. Coagulations force one's consciousness to focus on that one lower level of vibration, therefore multi-consciousness and effortless peace cannot be achieved and maintained, due to single-layered conscious focus.

Increased awareness/awakening

As we clear more and more of our coagulations of energy at the physical, emotional and mind levels of vibration it causes a variety of changes to slowly take place. As blocks are cleared this allows us to spend more time within the higher-vibration of heart-space, which brings an increased awareness within our energetic system. It also brings an increased awareness of our spiritual connection, and our connection to that which 'Is'. As the energetic system becomes clearer, we are more sensitive to other discordances. As we clear away more debris we can sense smaller and smaller, and deeper debris and issues. Often there are coagulations deeply embedded within our systems which we may not even be aware of. By unpacking and removing blocks and coagulations we will uncover deeper and deeper coagulations, which can originate from many years previously.

Often our current issues and concerns are built upon layer upon layer of discordancy, which usually stems from one initial experience or source. It is only when we begin to unravel and unearth these discordances that we can get to, and remove, the core issue or discordancy. Also, by clearing away the large discordances our energetic system begins to move more freely, and smaller discordances can be detected and resolved.

When our energetic system becomes more free-flowing it is easier to sense when things are not moving correctly within it, than when it is blocked or unbalanced in some way. If a pool of water is muddied it is difficult to see what is moving within it, or beneath the surface. The clearer the pool becomes, the easier it is to see what needs attending to within it. When our system becomes clearer, we become more sensitive to our own energetic disturbances and are quicker to attend to them. It becomes easier and quicker to identify and resolve things – to constantly keep clearing.

When our energetic system is clearer, we are also more able to sense which level of vibration our conscious gaze is sitting within. We are more able to sense our conscious gaze as it moves up and down levels of vibration. This makes it easier for us to focus on one layer at a time to work on different aspects of spiritual work. It also makes us more aware of what layer of vibration a discordancy sits within.

As our system becomes clearer, and we are living within heart-space, we become more sensitive to spiritual experience and guidance. This is because low-level coagulations are not blocking information being received by one's system. The information does not have to penetrate through layer after layer of debris to be noticed and received. Also, it becomes easier to decipher what is a real spiritual experience, and what are illusions created by the mind. A clear system allows one to feel the vibration of that which it senses. It becomes easier to decipher information by how it *feels*. It notices the precise clarity of spiritual experience, rather than the slightly cloudier vibration of that which is produced by the mind. It also makes it easier to sense when a spiritual experience is not of the 'light' or is a malevolent spiritual aspect masquerading as something it is not.

When the energy system is clearer, anything affecting it is flagged up more quickly and more clearly. Spiritual experience and information begin to become more frequent and of more use. When you can receive and listen more, the more useful the information you receive is to guide you on your path. But, do not become lost in the joy or wonder of spiritual experience. Spiritual experience is only a pointer towards your path to that which 'Is'. That which 'Is' should always sit firmly within the centre of everything you do.

When your energetic system is clearer, and you are more easily able to sit within heart-space, your connection to that which 'Is' is stronger and clearer. This is because heart-space connects you to the door to your soul, and within your soul sits the stronger connection to that which 'Is', through your own unique aspect of the divine.

So, in clearing and working with your own energy field, you are increasing your energetic system's sensitivity in many ways. All of which raise one's vibration and create changes which move us towards facilitating the integration of true soul-self. Clearing raises vibration. Raising vibration creates awakening. Whilst within heart-space we awaken to healing, love, interconnectivity, spiritual experience, and are more connected to soul and more consciously connected to that which 'Is' above. Also, the free-flowing movement and the stronger connection to our soul allows the flowing dynamic aspect of that which 'Is' to work through us, and we now have the clarity within our energy system to hear the Truth that this brings.

Energy field – stripped back to birth

One of the aims of clearing the energetic system and dissolving the three lower levels of vibration is to strip ourselves back to the purity and light that we were born with; to the unique blank canvas of you. You in authenticity and truth; your original pattern. You as the unique aspect of the divine that you are. To remove all behaviours, conditioning, experiences and created-self leaves us with our Truth. The truth of who we are, and what we have incarnated in this lifetime to achieve. All of us in some way are created, modelled, programmed or moulded from the second we are conceived. And to discover our truth, and the truth of what our role is here in this lifetime, we need to return to our state of purity, to be reborn in authenticity, truth and grace. To be returned to being in a state of a child is not regression, it is vigorous progression!

To examine, assess, dissolve, de-programme and take apart everything we believe ourselves to be, takes dedication and incredible courage. To truly dig into ourselves, and to dig up everything we have experienced and become, takes bravery and faith. We must go into some of the darkest and most perceivably unpleasant aspects of our own nature, and our worst and most painful experiences.

But we need to do this messy and most unpleasant job for us to cleanse, clear and progress on our soul's path. The harder it gets, the nearer you are to revealing your true light. Sometimes clearing our energy system and stripping back to our own truth and authenticity can be the darkest, ugliest and most painful of experiences. This goes on, and on, and on, the more you clear and uncover. But it is worth it, believe me. Therefore, the path can only be walked in love, faith, trust, truth, surrender, stillness and humility. Without these we cannot walk. We will all stumble and fall on this journey, and it is these that will pick us up and keep us walking.

The journey can be excruciating, as what tends to happen is that the more you evolve and uncover, spirit will present situations, feelings or people who will cause you pain, distress or reminders of past experience. These are presented to us, not for us to regress, but for us to progress. When we are working at coagulation and tethering resolving, and a painful situation presents itself to us, it is a blessing and a gift. It points us towards further work, further aspects of our created-self which need resolution. Use these experiences, situations and people as a conduit for growth.

Keep pushing through the pain to discover what is behind it. Once we understand what is behind the pain we can progress with further resolution. What we must not do is focus on the pain. If we focus on it, this draws us down into physical/emotional/mind vibration. This is what distracts us from moving towards the very nature of our own light and makes us become lost in incarnated human existence. If we focus on the experience of pain presented to us, we have come off our true path. Go behind the pain/situation, go beyond it. Find the disharmony and dissolve it.

Pain is a pointer, not a full-stop!

Although this is working at an energetic level, there may also be help and change required at a practical physical, emotional or mental level.

Perhaps you can do this alone, or with the help of family or friends, with members of your faith community or with professional help. The choices you make, are again, up to you, gauged by whatever you sense is right for you. You may or may not choose these individuals to hold your hand through your dismantling, but it is most important to remember this. It is you that must do it. It is <u>not</u> for others to do *to* you or *for* you. On your journey, the steps you take are your steps. Sometimes others may hold your hand, but it is you who walks. Each step is valuable, each leads you towards your own authenticity, each building you into your own truth.

Fear of losing self

As we work and work to dissolve all that we were, to discover and live authentically as all that we are, we hit another fear. And that fear is of losing who we are. This is very difficult for many people. Whether it be us ordinary folks, spiritual/energy workers or people of faith. If we dissolve everything that we are, what do we have left? Much of who we are we have created for ourselves, built upon the conditioning and programming we were given.

Sometimes we have created ourselves to be fabulous. We have done the absolute best that we can and lived the best life that we can. We have filled our heads with divine, albeit book-based, old-paradigm knowledge, and now we perceive we are being asked to smash it up and throw it all away. We have spent our whole lives creating who we are, and now we must dismantle it all. It leaves us naked and vulnerable, lost and lonely. It leaves us questioning who we are, what is our identity, what will I be if I remove my identity, my learning, my experiences, my position, my authority? What will I be left with? Who will I be?

When individuals begin to consider this there is often great fear and great anger. This fear and anger are quite rightly placed. When you have spent a lifetime building yourself, and are then asked to take it all apart, it can be difficult. But it is only in the taking apart that truth and growth can be accessed. It is not to say all that you know, have learned, have experienced, is of no value. Because it is. All these things can be used by you to help others and help yourselves. But instead of them defining you, they need to be put in your 'tool-box' to help others. Instead of these things *being* you, they are now *used by* you. They are gifts to be used and treasured, but they are not who you are. Use everything you have been gifted in life but understand that these things are not you. When you can put aside everything you believe yourself to be and stand naked, vulnerable, and alone, this is when you are closest to authentic soul-self, and closest to that which 'Is'.

When you believe you have lost you, you are closest to finding you.

This process is one of the ultimate tests of faith. This is when you truly walk in love, faith, trust, truth, surrender, stillness and humility. There are no short-cuts. There is no fooling yourself. You cannot buy your way to your soul-self and that which 'Is', and you cannot 'learn' your way to soul-self and that which 'Is'. Your position of authority, your greatness of mind, or expansiveness of wealth will not connect you to your soul or to that which 'Is'. Stripping back to purity and authentic truth is the only way.

But all that said, once this continual process is worked through, it may not mean that you are a whole different person. Aspects of the fantastic individual that you were will most likely remain, and they will be clear and true. If you understand that who you are has been built with the quiet whisper of soul guiding you, much of who you are, and your personality, will have the identity of soul throughout. But the process of taking apart and rebuilding ensures that all you are is authentic, clear, without coagulations, cords, ties, programming and conditioning. You will walk authentically as you, shining your unique 'light'. When you are stripped back to your purity you will be clear, free-flowing energetically, and of the heart-space vibration; this gives the perfect environment for your soul-self to incarnate or be 'reborn' within this lifetime, and your connection to that which 'Is' will be strong and incredibly beautiful.

Mel Cross

THE CORD OF LIGHT

*Conscious connection of
Sprit-self heart-space to
Soul-self*

Once you are living in your heart-space vibration, and you are working at dissolving coagulations from your energetic system and removing unnecessary cords and ties, you can work at the next stage of the evolutionary process.

But firstly, I must explain that all the things spoken of in this book are not necessarily linear. These stages and processes can happen simultaneously or independently of each other. Sometimes you are moving backwards and forwards between all of them. There are no set ways of achieving change and movement with these stages. Each of us is unique, all with different lives, experiences and circumstances. Your way of moving through these stages will be in the way that is right for you (even if it doesn't seem that way sometimes!) So, do not be disheartened if you lurch between sitting within heart-space, coagulation clearing, connecting heart-space to soul-self, and back again. Sometimes around and around in circles, sometimes appearing to go backwards, and sometimes seeming to have failed in every way. All of this is part of the process and to be expected. All of this will ultimately lead you towards your soul and that which 'Is'. It is not for us to decipher, understand, or make sense of. Everything is always leading us the right way, if it is done in love, faith, trust, truth, surrender, stillness and humility. Everything fluctuates, everything changes, and this is good. This indicates fluidity, and fluidity leads us the right way. Just go with it, and if that which 'Is' and love can be found in your heart, all will be well.

Connecting spirit-self heart-space to soul-self

At the centre of our heart-space, as we exist as spirit-self within our created-self, sits our connection to the essence of our unique aspect of the divine. Our light. Our connection to that which 'Is'. This light is corded up into the corresponding space within our soul. Within our soul shines brightly our unique light facet of the divine – our part of that which 'Is'. This facet is corded up through every layer of vibration, to the highest, purest vibration; to that which 'Is', above. Pure love. Pure light.

This cord of light can be sensed as running up through the channel of light, which also runs up through our energetic system, up through our crown, through every layer of vibration, and all the way up to that which 'Is'; highest vibration of love and light.

The channel of light is where our consciousness travels to each level of vibration to connect to, and work with, that layer of vibration.

The cord of light from heart-space spirit-self, connects to our unique aspect of the divine within soul-self, and cords us right the way up to the highest vibration of love and light – that which 'Is'. This cord that runs between heart-space, to soul, to that which 'Is,' is our unique connection to that which 'Is', above.

We are led to believe that we have to do certain things, have certain beliefs, or behave in certain ways to connect to that which 'Is'. But the fact of the matter is, we are always connected to that which 'Is', as our unique fragment of that which 'Is' resides within us and connects us to this most beautiful and wondrous thing ALWAYS. We may be distracted from this connection, we may have it clouded or blocked from our view, and at times we feel it is not there at all. But our light *always* shines at the centre of our being, and we are *always* connected to that which 'Is'.

Our disconnection is an illusion.

The truth always sits and shines quietly at our very core. It may be covered, but it is never extinguished.

What we sense, through this incredible connection, is the truth of that which 'Is'. This is where we sense the indescribable divinity of the light and love of that which 'Is'. Once this light and love have been truly experienced, it is the fuel and the catalyst for us to walk the path towards our soul, and our true connection to that which 'Is'. This love and light, once experienced, is the thing which inspires us, encourages us, loves us, holds us and carries us through everything which distracts us, hurts us, scares us, or shakes us from our path. It is the thing we hold firmly to when all else is disintegrating around us, and the darkness threatens to engulf us and snuff us out.

This light and love is ALL.

So, as we progress on our journey, it is imperative that we nurture, grow and encourage this connection. Once we are living within heart-space we are existing at the vibration at which we first glimpse this connection to that which 'Is'. This is why heart-space is so very beautiful. Once we become aware of our light sitting at the very centre of our heart-space, we can begin to strengthen the connection from our light at heart-space, to our stronger unique aspect of that which 'Is', situated at the centre of our soul. This is done by working tirelessly on the 'Principles of Connection' spoken of in an earlier chapter. If we can nurture this connection, we create a stronger link between our spirit-self and soul-self, and in turn our connection to that which 'Is'. When this link is focussed on, and consciously strengthened and worked with, the communication between spirit-self and soul increases, and our awareness of our own unique aspect of the divine also increases. We are more aware of communication between spirit-self and soul-self. We begin to sense our truth more, and who we truly are. We begin to feel more strongly the love and the light of that which 'Is'. We strengthen this cord of light purely by our conscious awareness of it. We can bring our consciousness to it, and feel its link between our spirit-self, soul-self and that which 'Is'. We also begin to sense the love that enters us from that which 'Is', and from our soul to our spirit/created-self. We feel divine love, and we begin to feel our love for ourselves.

This is important.

This cord of light is important, as it plays a crucial role in the incarnation of soul. When we live at the vibration of heart-space, dissolve our coagulations and unhelpful cords and ties, live strongly in love, faith, trust, truth, surrender, stillness and humility, and our focus is firmly on that which 'Is', the cord of light pulls true soul-self into incarnation in this lifetime.

As spirit-self ascends and reintegrates into, and within soul-self, the cord pulls soul into the heart-space. When soul integrates it sits at the vibration of heart-space, with your divine, radiant aspect of that which 'Is', shining brightly at the centre of it. The cord pulls your true light, and true soul-self, into fully incarnating in this lifetime. It is like our umbilical cord to that which 'Is'.

This cord of light, when developing, also helps bring us more spiritual information and connection. This is because, when developed, it creates a greater link to our soul, and soul can pass information more easily to spirit-self. As soul is multi-vibrational and a Dynamic Creator, it passes spirit-self that which it needs in order to evolve. As soul is in constant flow of dynamic, flowing, that which 'Is', it is in constant flow of information which can guide the spirit-self towards evolving. The stronger the link, the easier the information can be passed from one to the other. This stronger connection also helps us gain access to all that we have experienced, as every single moment we have experienced, and all that we know, is maintained beyond conscious memory, within our soul. When we have access to all that we have experienced we now move, sense and find more conclusions in a conscious way to our current situation, as we have endless information from the life we have experienced. We can access more answers, which in turn help us navigate our path ahead.

Our soul can pass information to spirit-self more easily and clearly, and our spirit-self is more able to receive and interpret the spiritual information and experience it receives. This is because spirit is one of the fluent languages between soul-self and spirit-self, and because we are more aware of, and comfortable with, the flow of dynamic, creative information and love from that which 'Is'.

But, as this cord strengthens, and our access to soul and spiritual information/guidance increases, we must ensure we are not distracted or overwhelmed by these incredible experiences. For even though they are incredible, they are only signposts helping us navigate our path towards integrating our soul and strengthening our connection to that which 'Is'. If we become blinded by, and lost in, spiritual experience and soul-self experience, we will never reach the unimaginable beauty and grace of that which 'Is' experience and soul integration.

Spiritual experience is incredible, that which 'Is' experience is beyond all things.

If we become distracted, lost or defined by our spiritual experience, we become as lost as those who have not even taken one step towards themselves. So many become distracted by, and lost in, spiritual experience, that they wander off the path to their soul and connection to that which 'Is' and progress no further. This is yet another way spirit ensures that those who travel the path towards that which 'Is' and soul integration, walk in love, faith, trust, truth, surrender, stillness and humility – the 'Principles of Connection'. If we keep these in our hearts always, we will keep upon the path. When we have incredible spiritual experience from the strengthening cord between spirit/created-self and soul-self, we must remember to say, 'thank you', and then let go of that which we have experienced. If we hold on to it, we define ourselves by it. If we define ourselves by it, we slip back into the vibration of mind and emotion. When we slip back into mind and emotion, we pull out of heart-space. When we pull out of heart-space, we lose the very connection which gave us the experiences in the first place.

Embrace, listen, learn, say thank you, let go and walk in humility. This way we are not distracted or pulled away from the true path we are to walk. This way, that which we experience points us towards our path, connects us to our soul, and this cord of light brings the light and love of that which 'Is' into the very depths and centre of our being. It helps us to connect to our truth, then helps us to integrate and live as our truth.

DYNAMIC CREATOR

Soul-self Incarnate

We have finally arrived at the potential destination of Dynamic Creator – Soul-self incarnate. If we are standing at the gateway to incarnating our soul in this lifetime we have worked hard and tirelessly at living within our heart-space, have dissolved our coagulations of energetic experience within our energy system, have created a strong cord of light between spirit-self and soul-self, and have been doing this with great strength and commitment to walking in love, faith, trust, truth, surrender, stillness and humility.

We have lived within heart-space, as this is the frequency at which the soul sits comfortably, as this is the frequency of love. We have expanded this space and made it more fluid by dissolving the low-level coagulations of energy within our system. This has created an energy system more free-flowing and love-filled, which is more comfortable for soul to sit within. It has returned us to our original 'pattern', which will eventually facilitate a harmonious merging of spirit-self and soul-self. And, we have strengthened the cord of light between spirit-self and soul-self, which connects them more fully and consciously, all of which prepares the spirit-self to integrate back into soul.

All the above should be done with love, faith, trust, truth, surrender, stillness and humility, as this is imperative to soul incarnation, and helps to keep us centred. If we do not sit in heart-space, clear our coagulations to create free-flowing movement of energy, and strengthen our cord between spirit-self and soul, we have not prepared our energetic system to integrate properly with our soul. Therefore, we will not be able to fully incarnate our soul. We will have created a much greater connection to it, therefore sensing that which 'Is' more fully, we will be receiving truth more fluidly, and we will be sensing our purpose more readily. We may believe we have fully incarnated, but what we have done is progressed incredibly, but not fully arrived. This is an achievement and of great merit in and of itself, but you will not be at your full potential.

It is love, faith, trust, truth, surrender, stillness and humility which will unlock your potential. Without them, no matter how hard you work, the door will not fully open. There is a reason for this, and it has been created this way to serve vital purpose.

Love, faith, trust, truth, surrender, stillness and humility are the links in the chain between us and that which 'Is'. They are the keys to unlock the twist in the energetic system between the spirit-self and the soul; the door between single-vibrational existence and multi-vibrational existence. Without full love, full faith, full trust, full truth, full surrender, full stillness (within flow) and full humility, all lived with full gratitude, the door (twist) stays closed.

The cord of light between spirit-self, soul and that which 'Is', threads through the centre of the twist keeping communication and connection at all times. This is where that which 'Is' can touch us, or soul and dynamic 'Is' can pass us 'truth' as a passive-receiver. It is the cord which we consciously focus on to receive information from spirit. This cord of light is our connection to that which 'Is'. This cord of light is our connection to our soul. This cord of light is, love, faith, trust, truth, surrender, stillness and humility.

There are reasons why the door between spirit-self and soul does not fully open until we have prepared our energy system for a new way of existing, and proven our commitment by working with love, faith, trust, truth, surrender, stillness and humility.

If we are not walking the true path we will:

- Not be consciously existing at heart-space. We will be visiting heart-space. We need to exist at heart-space for soul to incarnate. Soul does not sit comfortably with physical, emotional, mind vibrations as it does not contain these vibrations.
- Still be creating-low level coagulations as we will still be existing as ego; no matter how much we try to convince ourselves otherwise. Coagulations will not allow true fluidity in the energy system; fluidity is required for multi-vibrational soul-self to incarnate.
- Not have created a strong cord of connection between spirit-self and soul. The strong cord is created by walking the path with the Principles of Connection.
- Not be hearing the whole truth of our soul therefore will be working partly from mind, rather than from the unique aspect of the divine which we are.

The door between spirit-self and soul-self stays twisted until the above requirements are met and we are truly walking in love, faith, trust, truth, surrender, stillness and humility because:

- Our energy system needs to be ready.
- Our commitment needs to be true.
- Our love of that which 'Is' needs to be at the centre of all, and ever-present.
- We need to be working from soul-self and our unique aspect of that which 'Is'. This is so we incarnate our soul's purpose. And this must be done with purity and light.
- We must not, and CANNOT, incarnate our soul whilst being influenced by created-self/mind. To incarnate the potential of our soul, whilst sitting within created-self and mind, could potentially be disastrous. We would use our gifts for gain, control, hierarchy and growing our sense of 'me'. This is ego. Ego is destructive. To give ego the potential of the soul would

207

be devastating. Where there is destruction and ego there is potential influence from spiritual malevolence. Giving the potential of our soul to spiritual discordancy is not acceptable.

- The pain the soul would experience by the low-level coagulations and existence, if it connected to a cluttered energy system, would be horrendous. The three lower levels of vibration do not exist within the soul, they are discordant to it. They cause it great disharmony.

The twist in the connection between soul-self and created-self has been set up so that if there is anything other than purity and light in one's purpose, the twist will not open. No matter how hard one tries. You cannot fool your own soul! You can flog yourself, offer yourself and dedicate yourself, but without love, faith, trust, truth, surrender, stillness and humility, and purity and light in all, the door will not open. It cannot be forced. This is when we truly understand surrender. The more we want it, the more we must let go.

Therefore, you can put great effort into preparing yourself for soul incarnation, but without the keys of love, faith, trust, truth, surrender, stillness and humility, lived with gratitude, and in purity and light, the door will not be opened.

The process of soul integration

Although we talk of soul integration as a change at an energetic level, we will feel its effects throughout the process within physical, emotional and mind, as these are energetic frequencies. This is because we are living within a physical body, influenced by the emotions and guided by the mind. Therefore, it is imperative during this process to increase your sensitivity to energetic influences on your system and become increasingly sensitive to 'truth'. With the increases in your energetic sensitivity and your awareness of truth, you will be ever-able to discern between physical, emotional, and mind products, energetic influences, truth, spiritual guidance and experience of that which 'Is'.

When your system begins to change and prepare itself for its new way of being, we need to discern what is happening to us, and what we need to attend to, address, or ignore. Almost everything we experience and sense is guiding us, we just need to be able to decipher the information given to us.

We can experience many things whilst transitioning between created-self and soul-self, none of them are right, none of them are wrong. They just *are*. You may experience many symptoms, few or none. There are no set ways, we are all different and will experience things differently.

Some of the things you may experience are below:

- Tingles
- Rashes
- Aches
- Twitching
- Buzzing
- Feeling very hot
- Feeling very cold
- Headaches
- Foggy mind
- Light-headedness
- Crying
- Inexplainable mood changes
- Lights
- Shimmering vision
- Images
- Sensations
- Noises
- Very hungry
- Not wanting to eat
- Nauseous
- Unexplained changes in diet
- Extreme tiredness

- Sleeplessness
- Endlessly racing mind, especially in the night
- Suddenly needing to lay down and sleep (Feels like being 'turned off')
- Feeling extremely cold when 'turned off', not feeling like you can move
- Noticing how places/people 'feel'
- Noticing meaningful coincidences

All the above <u>can</u> be symptoms of illness, conditions and medication/drugs, rather than energetic changes. Always check with your doctor first if you are concerned about what you are experiencing. If the doctor can find no reason for the unexplained symptoms it may be that you are experiencing energetic change. But it is usually best to check with your doctor first to be sure, or if symptoms persist.

All the above indicators of energetic change, and preparation of one's energetic system, need to be consciously investigated by you. Therefore, you need to understand your energetic system, be able to work with your energetic system, be sensitive to what you are experiencing so that you can address it and be able to listen for *truth*. When we can discern truth, and are able to sense and decipher spiritual guidance, we will be supported and instructed through the process. We can work with what is happening to us, and because we can discern truth and sense the information we receive is coming from the right place, we can trust and surrender to the process.

The further along the path we walk towards soul-integration, the more extreme and frequent the symptoms may become. The more we trust and surrender, the easier we will be able to navigate the choppy seas! The tests will become bigger and often there are challenges so great, and times so dark, that our faith is tested to the point of breaking. But we must always remain focussed. This takes place for us to show nothing will shake or break our faith in that which 'Is'. It is our faith which pulls us through when we trust and surrender to the process, and when we sit within our knowing of that which 'Is'.

The integration of soul-self

Integration of spirit-self into soul-self, and the bringing down of soul-self to incarnate in this lifetime is experienced in different ways by different people. The physical experience of the returning of spirit-self to soul, and soul integrating, is felt in many ways according to the individual.

My experience was that I first sensed the clarity and fluidity of my energetic layers in a way I had not done before, after I had worked tirelessly to dissolve coagulated energy, cords and ties. As the fluidity increased, I noticed the free-flowing movement of my consciousness in a way that I had not felt before. My energetic field began to increase and become more and more greatly filled with love-vibration. I felt the loosening of my spirit-self within this, like it had become detached from, but within the energy system. I felt the expansion, fluidity and strengthening of the cord between the spirit-self and soul. Eventually, when the time was right, and all the criteria met, I was given the greatest, sometimes terrifying and darkest tests of faith. When I surrendered to that which 'Is', allowed guidance by Truth and trusted *fully*, the change then took place.

I sensed my spirit-self pull up into the centre of my soul, and my soul pull down into the larger, love-filled, created space, in my energy system. The spirit-self ascended via the cord of light, and it was the cord of light which pulled the soul into place. You will know when this has happened!! Trust me! It is euphoric, and there is a definite sense of being reborn. You are reborn fresh, new and ready to begin life again in the truth and light of your soul. It is the greatest and most humbling of gifts; a blessing from that which 'Is'.

Once this change has taken place it does take time to adjust to the new conscious way of living. There is a sense of going inside oneself to realise it is not a smaller space, but you have entered a door into the infinite. You realise that the inner you is, in fact, eternally expansive in every direction. The peace of the non-conflicting nature of multi-vibrational consciousness is indescribable. Being reborn as soul-self is a gift not only to oneself, but to all that 'Is', and to humanity itself. Treasure it.

Soul-self

When you incarnate as soul you have moved from living as a Passive Receiver, to a Dynamic Creator. You are no longer being directed and guided by your soul; you are living as your soul. This new way of being takes some time to adjust to, but it is an incredible privilege. You are no longer only guided on your path; you begin to become an active creator of your path. As you have now learned to keep that which 'Is' at the centre of everything you do, you live with and in love, and walk in humility and gratitude. Therefore, the path that you create is not centred around what is good for you, it is centred around that which is good for All. Your life is for the *we*, not the *me*, and this is when humanity begins to change. Your life grows with the truth and wisdom of that which 'Is', wrapped in the vibration of love and light.

When we incarnate as soul-self, Dynamic Creator, we now have access to the full illumination of our true-self divine spark. We fully recognise our facet of the multi-faceted divine. We feel our light shining deeply within the centre of our soul and we wish to share it with others, illuminate the way, and light the hearts and divine sparks of those around us. We wish to radiate, shine, and illuminate all, always. We realise, at last, that we too are the light.

Stop for a moment and reflect.

You know,
that you too,
are the light.

How incredible and humbling this is.
Never forget this.
Never lose your way or your focus on this.

Always be in awe and gratitude.

Always be the light you want to see in the world...

We now recognise that we are in full connection to, and recognise the fluidity of, our soul's purpose. We have an unshakably strong connection to, and understanding of, who we truly are and what our purpose is in this lifetime. This purpose is fluid and changeable, but when guided by *truth* we navigate it well. Our soul's purpose can find us making huge changes to ourselves and our lives, to best facilitate that which we are here to bring to humanity, but we make these changes, and sometimes sacrifices, with grace. We understand it is for the All, and we are gracious in our purpose. We work tirelessly with love, to bring our gifts, and understanding, with dynamic creation, guided by that which 'Is'. We are not afraid to work in new ways, as pioneers of growth, thought and being, to bring our strand of unique understanding to humanity. This strand can be in any discipline, from the complex, to the seemingly simple, to facilitate the changes humanity needs to move forward, in faith, with love, to evolve into the spiritual beings we are destined to become, and have always been. Each strand brought forward brings growth, renewal, understanding, support, illumination and light. And it is all brought with the flow of love from that which 'Is'. As pioneers of spiritual evolution, we walk with torches of light into the darkness of the old, in order to guide the way. Each strand of equal beauty and importance as the other. Together, in our unique ways, we work to create the tapestry of the whole. Each strand affecting the other, supporting the other, and working with the other, to become an illuminated One.

As we sit within our soul there are no longer boundaries between our connection to that which 'Is' above. We no longer have the cord from our created/spirit-self to our soul-self, and soul-self to that which 'Is' above. We sit within our soul-self and our unique divine aspect of that which 'Is' shines brightly at the centre of this. This divine aspect connects directly and strongly to that which 'Is' above, the constant emanator of love and light. We feel the flow of love and light from that which 'Is' above, deeply within us. We also flow our love back freely to it. This light and love fuel us in all we do and is shared with all. This flow of love and light flows from us and into all things, just by *being*. It is healing and illuminating at all levels for all things. We radiate and share this love and light always. This connection is strong, and as this cord of connection is our cord of faith, our faith is strong. We feel the light and love of that which 'Is' above, in everything we do, say and think, and in our very act of *being*. We sit within the centre of our divine aspect of 'Is' and are connected directly and strongly to the flow of love and light from that which 'Is' above.

When we are soul-self we also sit within the flow of dynamic, creative that which 'Is'. This dynamic flow of creation flows in us, through us and around us. As we are no longer Passive Receivers of information we are within the flow, rather than observing or waiting to receive the flow. This dynamic, creative, flowing, that which 'Is', is where everything comes from and returns to. It contains all that was, all that is and all that will be. It is the no-thing which contains all things, and it is in constant flow. This flow now moves freely through us as it is without barrier or constraint. As we are multi-vibrational, rather than single layers of vibration, there is freedom of movement. We no longer receive the creative flow; we are within the creative flow. Within this creative, dynamic flow of that which 'Is', is flowing 'Truth'. Flowing divine truth. This flowing truth is moving through us always. We no longer need to listen for, or receive, 'Truth'. We are within truth, and we recognise that truth. We sense flowing truth between the experiences, not the *facts*. We sit between the solidification of the facts, and within the flowing *knowing*.

We sit within the knowing of where we need to go, and what we need to do, for us to bring our soul's purpose into being in our everyday lives. The truth flows within us for us to dynamically create our individual truth. The individual truth of us, is a strand of the whole truth.

This is all possible because of our multi-vibrational existence. We are existing as all vibrations at once and sit within the knowing which can now flow freely through us. It is no longer blocked by low level vibrations, as these layers are now clear and fluid. These layers are also now the outer layers of our energy field, rather than the inner layers. They no longer cloud our vision or influence our view. Our light flows freely through our system and out into the world. Our light no longer must battle through the denser layers of vibration to be seen. It flows freely from the highest vibration, to the lowest vibration. It is no longer held captive within the denser vibrations, trying to find opportunities to flow out.

We now have one energy centre which contains all vibrations, and at the centre of this is our unique aspect of the divine light, which is connected to that which 'Is' above. We can separate these out to work at, or heal, specific areas or vibrational levels within ourselves, but they will return to one when the work/healing has finished. The 'One' energy centre drives all.

When we exist as soul we are multi-conscious, with all existing at once. Our consciousness no longer must move up and down vibrational levels to focus on an aspect of that which it wishes to explore. Consciousness exists at all levels of vibration simultaneously, and we sit peacefully within this. Flowing knowing moves through us and through our consciousness, rather than us consciously directing our gaze to it. Therefore, everything we need is accessible when we need it. If we sit in faith and trust, the truth is within us always. We do not need to hang on to this, own this, or categorise this (it is our old egoic mind and fear which would have us work in this way). We just need to *be*, and in that *being* we will have an awareness of all things.

We do not have the ability to process everything, nor would we want to. We do not require this, and our human brains do not have the capability for this. And this is good. We do not need to. We sit within the flow and know all will be as it will be, and all we need will be with us when we need it. If it is not with us, this is also good. It means it is not meant, and this is perfect also. Sometimes it is right and best that we are not aware of things. As a soul living a human life it is sometimes essential there are things we are not aware of. And we must always allow the guidance of truth, so that we do not influence that which we must not influence. We must remember respect and humility in all things. Only ego thinks it knows best over Truth.

Being within the flow is all that is required. This fluidity and letting go allows the real work to take place. It allows the freedom of that which 'Is' to flow in dynamic creation through us to realise our soul's purpose in this lifetime. And this is perfect.

With this multi-level consciousness, we are functioning at many levels of vibration at once. Sometimes we can be aware that we are working within several levels at once. Sometimes we are just aware that somewhere something else is going on, even though we are focussing our consciousness at one thing only. Both ways are ok; it just takes a little getting used to! Again, just *being* is all that we are required to do. To be part of the process, and not own the process. We will never be aware of levels we are not ready to receive, either we have not yet evolved enough to access them spiritually or would not be able to handle or understand them humanly. Either way this also is perfect. Although we are existing at all levels, we only consciously access the bandwidth to which we have evolved. Even though we have evolved to exist as our soul-self, our soul-self continues to evolve on its journey back towards returning to the love and light of that which 'Is' above.

Even when existing as our soul, we are still in the infancy of our spiritual evolution.

When we become our true soul, we may perceive that this will make us have a sense of feeling smaller as we are inward looking, rather than outward looking. This is absolutely not the case! To exist as our soul, we have a sense of infinite expansion. We sense ourselves expanding outwards into all things. Our vibrations are fluid and multi-vibrational, so we sense ourselves expand eternally outwards into the universe, and up and through all vibrational layers of existence. This may sound hard to comprehend, but it is a peacefully beautiful sensation.

It feels like we are breathing for the first time.

As we breathe, we expand outwards and upwards, in all ways to all places. The expansiveness is a sensation likened to all our atoms separating and expanding out in all directions, onwards and onwards and onwards. We sense our insignificance, and the greatness of our part in the Oneness, at the same time. It is truly magnificent.

This expansiveness and no-thing is easily accessed when in meditation and prayer, as we are now everywhere and nowhere. When closing one's eyes in meditation we are almost instantly in no-thing, sitting within the centre of that which 'Is'.

This is peace beyond peace.

As we are free-flowing between the layers of vibrational existence, we are also free-flowing along connections. This free-flowing connection allows us to flow with knowing to all people always. We are consciously connected to all, therefore we can bring truth to all, by allowing the divine, dynamic, creative flow to work through us. We are also able to share the light, love and healing given to us from that which 'Is' above. Through these connections we can illuminate, teach, and share, that which we sense. It is also through these connections that we can share our unique aspect of that which 'Is', and manifest and share our soul's purpose. As soul-self we can freely access all that we have learned and experienced, as it is now more freely accessible with the multi-vibrational consciousness. All learning, memories, and human experiences can merge with flowing-knowing to create understanding, and pioneering ways of thinking and working. We can access our subconscious storage as this is within the soul-self. By creating the freedom for access to all that we have experienced and learned, along with the flowing-knowing of divine dynamic creation, new and novel pioneering approaches and solutions to human and planetary problems will be achieved. There will be leaps forward in all areas, because we are now working with the flow, in ever-more creative and innovative ways, rather than in the stagnation of the set-in stone 'fact'. Facts are full-stops to dynamic creation. Dynamic creation should flow freely to keep bringing growth and movement. By being a conduit for this flow, we share that which 'Is' with *all*.

As soul we have an increased capacity for 'sensing'; both energetically and spiritually. This is because we are multi-vibrational and multi-conscious. We are free-flowing and connected to all. We can

217

receive guidance through the flow of knowing as well as from spirit. Spirit is more able to work with us as it does not have to communicate through the barriers of mind, emotion and physical. We sit within the vibrations which more easily communicate with spirit, and the translation process within us becomes ever-more efficient as it is used more often.

We become less attached to spiritual experience because we finally understand that it is to be lived with, rather than held on to or used to define ourselves. This is because we have changed our awareness from a physical being having an 'Is'-being experience, to an 'Is'-being having a physical experience. We are now living as a multi-vibrational soul, rather than a single-layered vibrational spirit/created self. We are now living both in the physical and spiritual dimensions at the same time. We no longer need to explain our spiritual experiences, because we are living a spiritually constant life, and this way of living becomes the normal way of existing. Spiritual experiences are transient, like physical experiences. We let them come and go and flow with them. We do not concentrate our gaze at them as we are always in the fluidity of these experiences. They come, they go, they inform us, they inspire us, they never cease to amaze us. But they are what they are, and they are always with us. This is not to say we are floating around in a cloud of spirit! But we are aware of the presence of that which cannot be seen, as part of our consciousness is also there. What we need to be aware of we will be aware of, that which does not concern us will not flag up. But what does happen is that when something does catch our awareness, we are able to follow the connection to see if we are required to act. When we are a Passive Receiver, we have information passed to us, or we consciously seek it. When we are a Dynamic Creator the information is fluidly around us and through us, only flagging up in our consciousness if it is necessary for us to take notice.

Our energy system becomes increasingly sensitive to vibrations at all levels, as we are conscious at all levels, and our consciousness becomes efficient at deciphering which disturbances to our energy need attention, and which do not. Which disturbances are flagging up information, and which are transient.

This flagging up draws our attention to disturbances and disharmony, both in people, places, situations and circumstances; both in the physical and spiritual realms. It helps us identify who/what needs help, attention, harmonising, healing or guidance. And when working with or within these people, places, situations and circumstances, we can sense when we are connecting properly to, and working correctly with, them, as we connect to, and receive from, these situations. We can sense the fluctuations in energy in these, and can flow with truth to bring harmony, healing, balance, peace and love in all ways to them. And because we work with love, faith, trust, truth, surrender, stillness and humility we do what we *know* is best (understood through dynamic, creative 'Is'), rather than what we *think* is best (created by mind). Sometimes our actions or words may not be understood, or even sometimes cause distress, but they are always the right thing, at the right time, to flow things in the right way. Sometimes this is only apparent later. Therefore, we must trust in the truth and guidance we are given. True words and actions which hurt, but heal, are always preferable to platitudes which sugar-coat but delay, or hinder, the true path to healing and growth. A good parent works with love and truth, rather than pacifying with misguided, hindering untruths.

Love in all thoughts, words and deeds; always.

This energetic sensitivity makes it much easier to identify our own personal energetic disturbances, which may go on to form coagulations if not addressed. It will also keep us working from the heart-space vibration of love, so that we can observe and efficiently deal with issues at a physical, emotional and mind level, with the guidance of truth. We can decipher why we are in disharmony, what's causing it, and how we can deal with this at a practical level. We are also able to decipher how we can harmonise the disharmony at an energetic level. We will be guided by our own sensitivity to energy as to whether what we are doing is working, and we are clear to be guided on the process of harmonisation by spirit and by that which 'Is'. We can listen without hinderance to the guidance of truth.

When we are existing as soul-self we work at all things from the point of truth, therefore we can make decisions and take actions guided by this. The decisions we make and the actions we take, if made from the point of truth, are often some of the more difficult things to do. As humans, the easy options are often not the right ones! When working as soul-self we always work from the point of self-less truth, as we know it is always guiding us the right way, even if the way can be perceived as 'wrong' or more difficult.

The path to the top of the mountain often means navigating boulders or grazing ourselves. But it is only when we gaze euphorically at the vista from the summit, do we realise the value of the pain and sacrifice it took to get there.

Also, when we exist as soul and are within the vibration of heart-space, we are in the constant vibration of healing. Therefore, when we are in situations or circumstances which cause us distress, we are a lot better situated to deal with them both practically and energetically.

When we sit within the vibration of heart-space, even if we are pulled down into physical, emotional, and mind, we quickly return to the position of love and multi-vibrational harmony. This is because we no longer require the resulting emotions or thoughts created by the event, as we no longer operate from ego. We do not need to 'own it'. We do not need to make judgements, we do not need sympathy, we do not require revenge, we do not need to define ourselves by the event, and thoughts and emotions which are a result of the event are far less able to coagulate on the outer surface of our energy system as they are so discordant to it. Discordancy flags up hugely and urges us to deal immediately with it to restore harmony.

Discordant energy is much less able to attach to our energy system. It needs to attach to the physical, emotional and mind layers, which are now free-flowing and clear, around the multi-vibrational soul. Single layer frequency coagulations often cannot attach to multi-vibrational energetic soul. Therefore, coagulations are rarer. They are also rarer because the soul sits within the vibration of heart-space/love, and soul is strongly corded to that which 'Is' above. Heart-space/love vibration is the vibration of healing (we are constantly at healing frequency) and we are flowing through our connection to that which 'Is' above, the constant emanator of love and light (healing). Therefore, our energetic system is constantly in the flow of healing vibrations, which are constantly harmonising disharmony, even when we are not working on it. We are instantly clearing our physical, emotional, mental and energetic disharmony, just by *being*.

Sometimes love-filled *being* is hard to understand by those still existing in single-vibrational created-self existence. They cannot understand our peacefulness and often non-reactive state of mind (although we do react sometimes – we are still human!). They also find it hard to comprehend our seeming lack of emotion to some situations. They think we do not 'feel'. The truth is we do feel the pain and emotion of things, in fact we feel it in an even deeper and stronger way, as we can feel the pain of not only our own emotions, but the emotions and effects of all around us. It is just that we return quicker to heart-space and work tirelessly to return to harmony. Not only for our own sake, but for the sake of those around us. We return quickly to heart-space, so that we can listen for *truth*, and deal with the situation in the best way possible. Also, so that we can dispassionately observe our human reactions, so that we can heal and harmonise ourselves at every level, and so that we can react in a truth-filled way, rather than a socially expected way. Sometimes people react en masse to an emotional situation and play out the reaction or role they perceive is expected of them. This is often not beneficial to them or to others and can often go on to skew the truth of a situation or inflame an already painful circumstance. By reacting from truth as a soul-self, we bring the truth, harmony, healing and love to all things regardless of what is 'expected'. And this will go part-way to helping illuminate the minds and hearts of others, when they experience/observe different ways of doing things and different ways of behaving. We must be the change we wish to see in the world around us, and this we can do by always walking in truth and love, to educated and offer possible alternatives to how humanity works at present.

Even when we exist as soul things can affect us so violently and painfully the wounds can run very deeply when they do affect us. But we strive to bring the truth of that which 'Is', with the love of that which

'Is', in a way that is bigger than we are. We carry and dissolve our pain as efficiently as we can, so that we can shine the light of love and healing in its place, for the benefit of others. We are also less emotionally reactive because as a dynamic creator our emotional layer of energy sits on the outer layers of our energetic system. Our light of consciousness sits further away from it at our centre. It takes a lot more for an emotional situation to create an emotional reaction.

We also, if guided by truth, absorb the pain of others into the outer layers of our energetic system, so that we can take away pain, and dissolve it with love, for their healing. We often do this without even being consciously aware of it (although at one level of consciousness we are aware, as we should not do what should not be done). Therefore, we need to be sensitive to our energy system, because we are connected to all things, we take on-board that which we can take away for others. This is so they can become clearer in their systems, so they can begin to raise their vibration, and hopefully begin to sense their own heart-space.

As I said previously, if I help you, I help me.

We are all connected.

We are all One.

The more we facilitate the environment for illumination and changes in individuals, the greater the effect of healing and illumination for humanity.

Reversal of soul-self

Existing as soul in human form needs constant observation, care and adjustment. You are always a work in progress. You are always in the fluidity and possibility of change. You will always face the challenges of life, but your tool kit to deal with them will be different. You are constantly in the process of evolution; the process is fluid and not static. Energy is always in motion, and always being affected by all things. Therefore, our most precious soul-self needs ongoing care and attention. Once we have achieved our 'goal' of existing as soul, things do not stop here. Our growth and evolution can continue, or it can slide backwards.

We have been given the magnificent opportunity to help not only ourselves but contribute to the spiritual evolution of humanity. We can bring peace, healing, light and love. We can operate from, and with, truth, to educate and illuminate. We can share the indescribable connection of that which 'Is'. We understand how to dissolve our created-self, how to work energetically for all, and how to clear our own disharmony and coagulations. We know how to listen for truth and how to be guided by spirit, our unique aspect of that which 'Is', the dynamic creative that which 'Is', and all wrapped within the light and love of that which 'Is'. But, should we stray from the fundamental principles of love, faith, trust, truth, surrender, stillness and humility, and we no longer feel gratitude as we walk our path, our soul may retreat.

Life will test us. Life happens. We are human. If we do not work with the gifts we have been given, following the fundamental principles, we will go backwards. Our conscious gaze may stay too long within the physical, emotional and mind levels. We may begin to define ourselves by our new-found awareness. We may begin to form a new created-self and begin to slip into the realms of ego. As we reverse we will create disharmony, we will begin to reform our more rigid layers, and we will begin to create coagulations. We will lower our vibration, cloud our vision, and be drawn out of heart-space existence. When this happens soul will retreat, and spirit-self will return. The twist between them will reform.

We are most arrogant if we perceive that we can abuse the gift of soul-self without consequence. If we abuse, we are lost. We return to single-layered existence and must work hard to achieve soul-self incarnation again.

But this can be done, I am sure, if we walk the path once more.

Soul and enlightenment

As our soul we have been sitting with the flow of divine dynamic creative 'Is' flowing through us. This brings us the possibilities of enlightened thinking and understanding. But this is not enlightenment. What we are doing when we are existing as soul-self incarnate is preparing our energetic system for the next stage of existence. This is where we exist as an enlightened soul.

As soul-self incarnate we sit at the vibration of heart-space/love and are a fluid conduit for our unique aspect of that which 'Is', the dynamic creative that which 'Is' and the constant emanator of love and light that which 'Is'. We do all of this via the supporting principles of connection; love, faith, trust, truth, surrender, stillness and humility, all with deepest gratitude. We work to exist in a constant state of truth, love and light. All of which create the perfect environment for the next stage of evolution; enlightenment.

Enlightenment works very much like soul integration.

Enlightenment is gifted to us from that which 'Is' above. Through our unwavering love, our selfless, tireless work, and our total dedication, walking fully in love, faith, trust, truth, surrender, stillness and humility, we have shown our commitment, our love, our unfailing trust and our dedication. We are living at the frequency of love and as our own truth. No matter what our life, or thoughts, bring us we do not falter. No matter how we are tested physically, emotionally, mentally or spiritually, we do not falter, even when these tests are extreme. We do not take our focus from the light of that which 'Is', the light at the centre of our being, and the light of knowledge from the creative, dynamic that which 'Is'. These things hold us unshakably, and unmovably, in the divine light of Truth.

We are living as our own unique facet of the divine and we are living true to this, bringing all that this unique light has gifted us, and sharing that gift throughout our life, and through all that we do. We have, working through us, the divine dynamic, creative, flowing truth of that which 'Is'. And we have the light and love of that which 'Is' above, flowing into us always. All of which create an environment for that which 'Is' above, to incarnate with the unique aspect of that which 'Is' within you, and the dynamic, creative, that which 'Is' which flows through you.   This coming together into a conscious, physical incarnation, when the three become one, is enlightenment.

We cannot influence this, nor strive for this. We sit, allow, wait, and open, with patience, gratitude and love, within the silence of our being. When, and if, we are ready, all that we are enters that which 'Is' above, and that which 'Is' above pulls down into us, via the cord of light.

This is when we live with the divine truth and light of the three, as One, within us.

This is enlightenment.

HOPE

Love

We believe we live in a world full of despair and destruction, of pain, corruption and greed. A world where the hungry go unfed, the vulnerable go unheard, and the conflict between peoples at all levels of existence, and in all places, rumble on like blackest thunder. A world where the air, water and earth of the planet are polluted and ravaged, the trees slashed down, and the animals crushed. A world of pain, a world of disharmony, a world of hate. A world where corruption and poison has spread and seeped into every area of life, everywhere that we look, spreading silent and unseen. A world, some say, which cannot be helped, cannot be saved and cannot be put right.

People do not know how to help, do not know how to change, do not know how to bring the light back into all things. They hide within their lives, and their created worlds, and do not wish to see the truth of that which threatens us all. We have been blinded to our ability to make a difference, to see a different way, to be the difference. We have lost our ability to connect to our truth, the world's truth, the truth of that which 'Is'. We have lost sight, lost direction and worst of all lost hope. The hope that things can change. The hope that the sun, one day, will shine again.

But there is hope. There always has been. There always will be.

It is the glimmering wisp of light in the blackest of places. It is contained within the beat of our heart and each breath that we take. It is the movement of love within all things, between all things, and through all things. It has always been there. It will always be there. Because it 'Is'.

We all contain this movement of love, it is within us, through us and around us. And, if we can remove the blindfolds placed upon us and begin on the journey towards the truth of us, we can begin to embody this love, share this love, and be this love. The time has come to not look outwards for what needs to change. The time has come to no longer point the finger of blame outwards, but to point it inwards, to direct us to our truth. The truth which will make a difference, a truth that has been gifted to you to grow, to share, to bring to the table.

We may not be able to change the world on our own, but we can be the change we wish to see. We can embody the change, be the change, do things differently, and light the way. Light the way for others. Light the beacon of hope. Not alone, but together.

I hope this book has challenged your thinking, rattled your foundations, and shaken you awake, even if only a little. I hope it has made you question, ponder, and feel. I hope it has held your hand as you begin to explore your feelings, your thoughts, your spiritual understanding, and most of all your path towards your true-self and your truth. And ultimately held your hand as you stepped towards the mystery of that which 'Is'.

Some things you may agree with, some things you may not. It really doesn't matter, as long as there is movement, and with the movement comes the flow, and the flow will bring illumination.

It is not for me, nor anyone, to preach to you the right way or the wrong way. Right or wrong are judgements, and judgement comes from the mind, not the heart. But it is for us to offer possibilities, and for us to shine a light into the corners you haven't yet explored. How you explore and what you discover are up to you, as each path is unique. Maybe you will take one step, maybe you will walk for the rest of your lives, it is all as it should be. Even one step may be the very step that makes the difference, tips the balance, creates the change. Your one step might be all that we need.

That which you seek is within you. You need look no further. Connect with it, live in it, and bring it here to share with all.

Take time to help others, to see the beauty and value in all things, to embrace yourself. Take time to be present, to bring joy, to share your Truth.

Never give up hope, never let your heart be closed by the illusion, never stop shining.

For it is up to us now. Together. All of us.

The sun will shine again...

And the warmth, and the light, of that sun,

is

Love...

ABOUT THE
AUTHOR

Sometimes we experience things which are beyond rational explanation within this physical, emotional and mental experience of ourselves and our world. It is only when we stretch between and beyond this, that we begin to sense the *more*, the wonder and the *whole*.

Through experience and circumstance, so much of which I am unable to share, my being and my life changed. I have always been sensitive to people, animals and place, and I have always sensed spirit and spirits. But I have always questioned, always rationalised, and always tried to keep my feet on the ground. I have tried to help, heal, care for and love, as best I could, everyone and everything around me. But there was always something missing. And that something, I now know, was understanding the connections which flow it all together, that I was living as a part of, with, and through, that which 'Is'.
Living as an 'Is' being through the medium of a 'human' being.

I find it difficult to describe myself. As everything I was, everything that defined me, every experience I had before I became my 'truth' no longer defines who I am. It is in losing my created-self, the describable part, that I found my true-self, soul-self, and my unique facet of that which 'Is'. When you begin to understand that you are everything and no-thing, it becomes impossible to find words to express that which you sense you truly are. This is not egotistical, self-absorbed nonsense, it is, in fact, the opposite! To define solidifies descriptions and energy, to be in non-definition maintains flow and growth.

The understanding and process shared in this work was brought into my conscious awareness after years of trials and testing through many, many extensive and extreme spiritual experiences, both positive and negative. It was brought into my awareness from flowing that which 'Is', by walking in love, faith, trust, truth, surrender, stillness and humility, and because I listened...

For the moment I don't share my personal spiritual journey. This is because the work contained within this book should connect with your mind, stir your emotions and resonate deeply within your heart and soul by its own merit. You should see it, hear it and sense it via the deepest connection to love and light from which it came. It stands and speaks to you one to one, from that which 'Is' to your unique facet of that which 'Is'. My experiences and journey may cloud and sway that which you read as it may pull you into your mind, into judgement, into stagnation and into non-flow.

For example, here are some labels which may help you connect with your mind:

British
Female
40's
University Educated
Teacher – Primary school
Animal carer and behaviourist
Artist
Author
Healer – People, animals, places, spirit
Spiritual Guide

Yuk! Now scrunch them into a ball and throw them all away. Labels may create instant judgement, definition and compartmentalising according to your own perspective and experience. Writing these labels made me very uncomfortable indeed, because they are not descriptions of my eternal truth, soul-self, they are transient descriptions of created-self experiences within this lifetime. They are items of clothing worn, changed, disposable, but they are not my skin.

My spiritual experiences, like my physical experiences, are transient, and are not worn externally to describe, explain, nor define that which I am.

We are black, we are white, we are male, we are female, we are light, we are dark, we are everything and no-thing. We are neither one thing, nor the other. If we are one thing or the other, we create separation within ourselves which causes conflict. Therefore, when we recognise we are all things and no-thing, in a constant state of flux and change, within the *flow* of us, we find our peace.

That which 'Is' cannot be compartmentalised, owned, described or labelled. And we, as unique facets of that which 'Is', cannot be compartmentalised, owned, described or labelled. That which 'Is' is everything and no-thing, as we too are everything and no-thing. We live within the all, through the all, *and* as a unique facet of the all.

There are infinite ways of expressing this and sharing this, as there are infinite ways of walking the path as part of, with, and through, that which 'Is'. This work is my unique experience and understanding. It is neither right, nor wrong. It just *is*. It is truly about my promise to share that which I was made aware of, so that you too can experience and live as the blessing that is that which 'Is'.

This work is a sharing of possibilities. It is for you to sense and ponder, it is for you to feel. It cannot be forced upon you, nor dictated to you. It is only through freedom of thought, sensing and expression, and through your own experience, understanding and circumstance, that the resonance of that which has found expression here can be felt and experienced. This work is to promote discussion, create links, and build pathways of friendship and communication between people, disciplines, and ideas. It is to help energetic flow, illumination and communication of how we can change, and how we can be the change. By practical application of both ancient knowledge and understanding already with us, and new knowledge and understanding being brought to us at this present time, dynamic links between people, ideas and disciplines can create new pathways, new ways of working, new understanding, and help to create the new world.

Therefore, it is not about me as an author or creator, it is about you as a creator within the dynamic, creative, flow of that which 'Is'. You are the author of your own story, you are the walker of your own path, your truth is your destination. You are a unique facet of that which 'Is', as am I. I cannot be you, and you cannot be me, but that said, we are the same. I am you and you are me. We are different expressions of the One, and we are both parts of the Whole.

It is not important that you know who I am, but it is of utmost importance that you know who you truly are, your truth, your soul-self.

So, with deepest respect for all, and for that which 'Is', find the truth of *you* my beautiful friend, and shine...

With deepest love and blessings,

Mel x

And, just for the record, I love music, I dance, I sing (loudly!), I goof about. I love, I laugh, I cry... I am a mother, a daughter, a sister, a lover, a friend. Sometimes I eat rubbish, sometimes I shout, and I laugh, a LOT!! I fall over, I get things wrong and I can be very naughty! It is all good. It is all as it should be. We are all perfectly imperfect... It is a gift to be human... We are here to live our facet of 'Is' in human form... So, as we journey through the process from Passive Receiver towards becoming Dynamic Creator, remember this...

Let's celebrate this gift of life and enjoy ourselves too! Always laugh, always have fun, always hug, always love, and always, always be you...

...an utterly fabulous human 'Is' being.

Please share this book with others; whether they are like you, or different to you.
You never know whose heart is ready...

Printed in Poland
by Amazon Fulfillment
Poland Sp. z o.o., Wrocław

48965501R00141